80 FIVE-MINUTE GOLFLESSONS

80

FIVE-MINUTE

GOLF
LESSONS

COMPILED B
THE EDITORS
OF
GOLF DIGES
MAGAZINE

FROM
THE WORLD'S
GREATEST TEACHING
PROFESSIONALS

A GOLF DIGEST BOOK

INTRODUCTION

FOR MANY YEARS we at GOLF DIGEST have been aware that it is difficult, if not impossible, to benefit from vast amounts of golf instruction at one sitting. An overdose of instruction can easily prove fatal to one's golf game.

Our editorial policy for major instructional articles in GOLF DIGEST Magazine is to offer no more than four or five well-illustrated key points in a single feature. The objective is to leave readers with a few concrete thoughts that will help them to play better, rather than countless gems of extraneous wisdom.

Another important part of our instructional format is the one-page "Reminder" which first appeared in GOLF DIGEST in the late 1950s. Each GOLF DIGEST Reminder is nothing more than a five-minute golf lesson designed to leave the reader with one thought. They deal with fundamentals about the golf swing, strategy, practice, and rules.

Most of the GOLF DIGEST Reminders come from *teaching* golf professionals as opposed to *playing* professionals. We feel that these teaching pros, who encounter daily the swing problems of amateurs of all shapes and abilities, are best suited to offer instruction in the Reminder format. By simply asking these professionals, "What piece of advice have you found most helpful for those who come to you for lessons?", we have derived a series that has really been of practical value to average golfers.

These Reminders have been born in many different ways — through phone conversations with various pros, or over a tape recorder, or a post-round drink, and, of course, during an actual game. For instance, in June of 1965 I was slicing badly during a friendly round with Buck Adams, pro at the challenging Country Club of North Carolina. After watching me for several holes, Buck passed along a simple and very helpful piece of advice about positioning myself properly at address so my shots would go straight. Buck didn't realize it at the time, but he had just contributed another GOLF DIGEST Reminder. You'll find it in this book on page 17.

In this volume, we have included 80 Reminders. Some of them have appeared over the years in GOLF DIGEST Magazine. Others have been prepared specifically for this book. These 80 five-minute golf lessons have been categorized into instructional chapters covering nearly every phase of the game.

I would use this golf instruction book in two ways. First, I would browse through it simply to refresh my memory about key fundamentals that I might have overlooked recently. I would seek out only those basics that have proved helpful to me in the past.

Second, I would use this book as a reference work any time when my game went sour. For example, if I were having trouble with sand shots, I would check the Table of Contents under "Trouble Shots" and see what lessons are included that will help me get out of sand better. It's quite probable that one of these lessons would give me the results I sought.

I do not suggest that you experiment with those lessons that deal with parts of your game that are already working smoothly. That would be like bringing a perfectly healthy automobile to a garage for repair work. In the case of your golf game, such experimentation more often than not leads to new weaknesses.

80 FIVE-MINUTE GOLF LESSONS represents the "favorite piece of advice" of dozens of the world's outstanding professionals. We at GOLF DIGEST feel that their lessons will serve you well in the years to come.

RICHARD AULTMAN
Editor, GOLF DIGEST
Norwalk, Connecticut
December 1967

TABLE OF CONTENTS

80 FIVE-MINUTE GOLF LESSONS

THE ADDRESS

Care about your address position helps guarantee that the clubhead will return to the correct position at impact. Conversely, it is pretty much agreed by most teaching professionals that most mistakes made by average golfers stem from a bad address. They have found that with limited adjustments of the address position, golfers with erratic slices, hooks, and other maladies that hurt their score have been able to hit the ball longer and straighter.

Addressing the ball begins with the placement of the clubhead on the ground and continues through assuming the grip posture and stance. Your address is set when you are ready to put your swing into motion. The proper execution of each address element is critical to a good golf shot.

When placing the clubhead on the ground behind the ball, the sole of the club must lie flat. Should the outer or inner part of the clubhead be raised, there is a good chance that the resulting shot will be poor.

A proper grip is essential to any golf shot. The correct placement of your hands on the club guards against the club slipping during the swing. It also gives you the flexibility you need in your wrists and provides the best combination of clubhead speed and control over the alignment of the clubface. If you have the proper coordination, your grip will help you get power and accuracy from your swing.

A proper posture at address provides a "suspension point" at the base of your neck that remains constant throughout your swing. This is the center of your swing arc. Throughout your swing your body will rotate around this suspension point.

The basic stance requires that your weight be concentrated on the balls of your feet and equally distributed between your feet. Let your arms hang naturally, with your wrists straight. The left arm is essentially straight at address, but the right should be bent slightly, with the elbow close to your body. Both knees are flexed, not locked, and your back is straight but slightly tipped forward from the waist.

The lessons in this section cover specific aspects of the address position. They are mainly general reminders to help you develop the foundation of a sound golf swing.

SQUARE OFF AT 90°
FOR STRAIGHT SHOTS

THE ALIGNMENT OF the hips and shoulders directly affects the path of the clubhead.

To properly position your body, follow this routine:

First, sight an imaginary line from ball to target.

Second, sight another imaginary line, from the ball to an object on the right side of the fairway. These two imaginary lines should form a 90-degree angle at the ball.

Third, assume your addesss position while directly facing the object you have selected at the side of the fairway.

Fourth, finally glance down the target line for confirmation.

This will encourage your taking the club away from and returning it on a path along the target line.

by BUCK ADAMS

PROFESSIONAL, COUNTRY CLUB OF NORTH CAROLINA, SOUTHERN PINES, N.C.

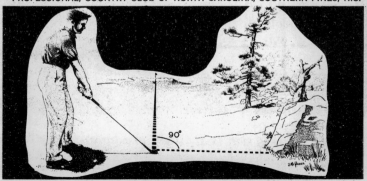

*Pointing your chin to the right at address will re-
move the tendency to rotate your head during the
backswing. Although your head is to the right, keep
your left eye on the ball at address (dotted line).*

POINT CHIN
TO RIGHT FOR
STEADY HEAD

Your HEAD snould remain in a steady position — behind the ball — throughout your swing. It may turn slightly with your shoulders, but any up, down or sideways head movement may throw your clubhead out of a proper path. This results in mis-hit shots.

You can protect against head movement by pointing your chin slightly to the right just before you begin your backswing. Concentrate on looking at the ball with your left eye. This "pre-turning" of your head minimizes any further need to move it during your backswing. It will also help you make a full shoulder turn for maximum build-up of power.

by GENE SHIELDS
PROFESSIONAL, LAKE WACO GOLF COURSE, WACO, TEX

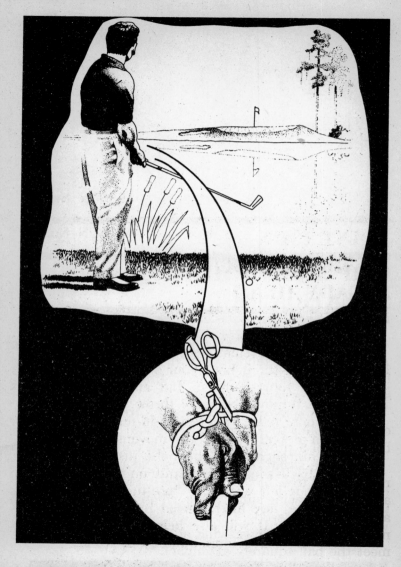

Your grip should always feel firm yet not tight. A good guide to follow is to imagine that a rope binding your hands has just been cut.

GRIP LIGHT WHEN SITUATION TIGHT

A GOLFER HAS a tendency to tighten his grip when faced with a tense and challenging shot situation, such as a long carry over water.

Tightening his grip, particularly with his left hand, causes a golfer to stiffen his wrists and jerk his clubhead out of a proper plane. Mis-hit shots result.

In tense situations, consciously keep both hands relaxed and free, but firm enough to control the club, as your backswing starts. This will give you a smooth and rhythmic swing. Your left hand will tighten naturally on the downswing and your clubhead will meet the ball squarely at impact.

by **JOE NOVAK**
PROFESSIONAL EMERITUS, BEL AIR COUNTRY CLUB, LOS ANGELES, CALIF.

Crouching will put your hands much lower at address (top) than they have to be at impact (bottom). The adjustment you'll make often is the cause of a "topped" shot.

STAND 'TALL'
TO AVOID
TOPPED SHOTS

THE TOPPED SHOT, which skitters along the ground after the ball has been struck above its center line, is often caused by bending the knees too much at address.

Sometimes a golfer will crouch so much at address, in an attempt to avoid topping the ball, that he then straightens up as he makes his backswing.

This lifts his hands and clubhead so that, if his legs remain straightened on his downswing, his clubhead will strike the ball above its center.

If you top shots, try "feeling tall" when you address the ball. Your knees should bend only slightly. Standing tall at address will eliminate the tendency to lift the clubhead out of its proper path, the end cause of topped shots.

by KYLE BURTON
PROFESSIONAL, THE OLYMPIC CLUB, SAN FRANCISCO, CALIF.

CORRECT

INCORRECT

ALIGN LEFT HAND
WITH SQUARE
CLUBFACE

MAKING SQUARE contact with a clubface that is looking at the target during impact is very important in producing straight shots. Offline shots are often caused by a clubface that is opened or closed, looking right or left respectively, during impact. If your clubface is "square" on the backswing, it will probably return to the ball squarely.

You can check for a "square" clubface midway in your backswing by noting the direction in which the back of your left hand and your clubface look. Both should be aligned in the same relationship as achieved in the address position.

When your hands are hip-high on your backswing, the back of your left hand and your clubface should be facing forward (see correct drawing on opposite page). If the back of your left hand is looking at the sky, you have rolled your clubface into an open position. If it looks toward the ground, you have a closed clubface.

To achieve a "square" clubface throughout your swing avoid any independent rolling of your hands and forearms during your swing. Your hands and arms should move as a unit in conjunction with the tilting and turning of your shoulders and hips.

by L. A. WELCH
PROFESSIONAL, RALEIGH (N.C.) COUNTRY CLUB

If your feet are no farther apart than the width of your shoulders, you can surely achieve the right hip turn and the transfer of weight on both the backswing and the downswing.

SPREAD HEELS
SHOULDER WIDTH

THE FEET ARE BASICALLY the platform for the golf swing, yet many amateurs overlook this relatively simple principle. One of the most common errors is placing of the feet too far apart at address. This creates tension in the legs and inhibits the golfer's hip turn on the backswing. It also reduces the effectiveness of his footwork on the downswing and robs him of power and rhythm.

A proper stance finds the feet spread about shoulder width — as measured by the outside of the heels and outside of the shoulders — at address (see illustration on opposite page). Ask a friend to check this relationship, or do it yourself by looking in a mirror. This stance encourages your legs to bend slightly at the knees, helps you achieve a good hip turn, and allows a smooth transfer of weight through proper footwork. Good footwork helps create dynamic balance during the swing so that maximum power can be released in the hitting area.

by PAUL ERATH
PRESIDENT, PGA SENIORS

Before starting your swing, check (1) the club alignment with the target, (2) your grip, (3) the extension of your arms, and (4) the positioning of your feet.

UP THE ARMS, DOWN TO THE FEET

Y OU WILL PLAY more consistent golf if you develop a systematic method of lining up and preparing to swing. After deciding what club to use and what type of shot to hit, I recommend a four-point checkup before you swing.

1. Check the grip. Are the palm sides of the hands lined up with the clubface?

3. Extend the arms to a comfortable — not stiff — position.

4. Widen the stance to the proper width. It will aid your balance if your feet are about as wide apart as your shoulders on full shots. The shorter the shot, the narrower the stance.

The thought pattern is from the ball up the hands and arms, and then down to the feet. This makes it easy to remember — up the arms, down to the feet.

Address position faults can ruin a shot before the swing begins. So develop this four-point check list. It will add consistency to your game.

by JACK KOENNECKER
PROFESSIONAL, CANYON C.C., PALM SPRINGS, CALIF.

THE SWING

Many tournament professionals and leading amateur golfers find it helpful to concentrate on a single position or action during the swing. By doing so, they have smoothed the way to an effective overall game.

Dave Marr, a former PGA champion, is one who holds to this premise. Admitting that he doesn't want to "clutter his mind" with a lot of details, Marr says that when he works on a single phase — for instance, swinging the right palm through so that it faces the target in the hitting area — he is usually successful in correcting other faults he may have developed.

To this end, it is good advice for the average golfer to read through all of the swing lessons that follow. Study them, every one of them, but execute and practice only one at a time. All of the points the lessons make are separate items that together make up a coordinated and powerful golf swing. They are designed to mesh. In fact, they are listed in the sequence in which they affect the swing, with the waggle beginning it all and a high finish completing the section.

If you feel you are having difficulty in a certain phase of the swing, select those lessons which cover your problem. Take this information to the practice tee before going onto the course.

Does your backswing feel awkward? There are five lessons about this part of the swing. If you apply any one of them there is an excellent chance that everything else will fall in place, since backswing faults often cause problems later in the swing.

Perhaps you are losing power or direction on the downswing. There are three lessons on how to start the downswing. Don't make the mistake of trying to think of all three as you begin your move back to the ball. Pick one out — the other two will come naturally.

Four lessons are concerned with action at the impact area. Start working with these movements in slow motion. They happen so quickly in the swing that it would be difficult, at best, to learn them at full speed. Gradually step up the tempo until at last you are swinging at the normal speed. The same advice could apply to the lessons regarding post-impact phases of the swing.

You may be surprised to learn tha once you have developed the correct application of just a few elements of the swing, the rest of the movements will fall into place automatically.

GOOD WAGGLE
DUPLICATES TAKEAWAY

A GOOD WAGGLE, the preparatory movement of your clubhead behind the ball as you take your stance, serves not only to test your aim, but also can help you develop a smooth, well-coordinated takeaway on your backswing.

Actually, the waggle should more or less duplicate your takeaway (see left illustration below). Your hands, arms and body should move together as a one-piece unit.

The clubhead should not waggle up and down behind the ball (see right illustration below), a familiar method of novice players. This up-down waggle might cause you to lift the club abruptly on your takeaway.

The waggle frees tension, keeps you loose, and overcomes inertia, unlocking you, so to speak, for the takeaway. It also gives you the feel of the rhythm of the prospective shot.

by JIMMIE GAMEWELL
PROFESSIONAL, HOGAN PARK GOLF COURSE, MIDLAND, TEX.

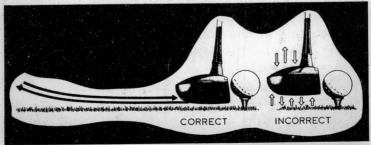

CORRECT   INCORRECT

ESTABLISH SMOOTH TEMPO DURING TAKEAWAY

IN STRIVING for extra distance, many golfers tend to swing harder and faster, relying too heavily on their arms to produce power. As a result, they destroy their timing and actually lose distance. Establishing a smooth, unhurried tempo in your backswing can help you avoid rushing your shots and wasting power.

The tempo for the backswing is set during the takeaway, the first 12 to 18 inches the clubhead travels away from the ball. Your takeaway should be low, slow and smooth. It should be a "one-piece" movement as your hands, arms and body move together as one unit.

by PAUL LEMCKE
PROFESSIONAL, TUCKAWAY COUNTRY CLUB, MILWAUKEE, WISC.

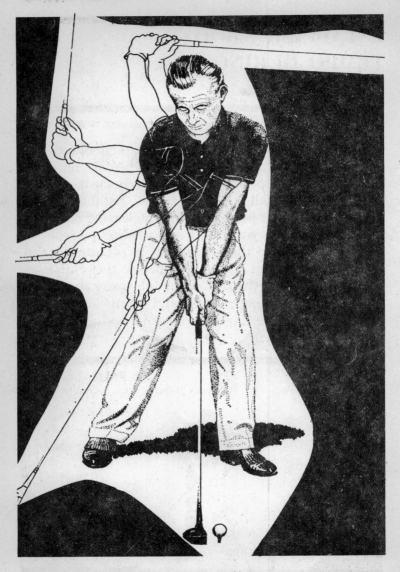

Note that throughout the backswing, the left arm is fully extended although the right arm bends slightly. This extension results in a full swing arc.

EXTEND LEFT ARM FOR FULL WIND-UP

As you fully coil your body on your backswing, you stretch the muscles of your left side. This gives you a slow build-up of power, much like an archer achieves when he pulls the drawstring on his bow.

To achieve a full wind-up with a maximum stretching of left-side muscles, make sure your left arm is extended, but not rigid, both at address and throughout your backswing.

With your left arm fully extended, you should feel that you are taking the club back as high as possible to the top of your swing. Do not, however, sway or lift your head or your body in attempting to make a full backswing.

Full extension of the left arm during the backswing, not only fully stretches the left-side muscles, but it also widens and lengthens your swing arc, another factor that will help you generate maximum clubhead speed through the hitting area.

by ROBERT HALSALL
PROFESSIONAL, ROYAL BIRKDALE GOLF CLUB, SOUTHPORT, ENGLAND

Overswinging can ruin a golf shot because it destroys proper timing. The golfer on top has broken his wrists too soon on the downswing. The golfer on the bottom has swung within his power and his arms have correctly returned to his right side before his wrists begin to uncock.

SWING WITHIN YOUR POWER

BACK IN THE OLD DAYS I played in a tournament with Macdonald Smith, one of the great masters. His advice was, "Son, you're going to have to learn to swing with 80 or 85 percent of your power. This will preserve your timing. On the short seventh hole to-lay, what did you use?"

"A 6-iron," I said.

"Didn't your ball hit the green and bounce over?" he asked.

"It did. What did you use, Mr. Smith?"

"A 3-iron. Did you notice how my ball carried to the green, landed and sat down just like a poached egg? Whenever in doubt use a little longer club and swing within your power."

The average golfer often underclubs himself. He delights in making a 5-iron shot go as far as the other fellow's 4-iron shot, and loses control. Swinging with 80 or 85 percent of your power isn't swinging slowly. It's fast enough to give you plenty of distance and preserves your timing — your wrists tend to uncock later in the downswing, promoting both distance and accuracy. The golfer who tries to kill the ball tends to release his wrists too early, losing clubhead speed and throwing the clubhead out of the proper swing arc.

by **WIFFY COX**
PROFESSIONAL, CONGRESSIONAL COUNTRY CLUB, WASHINGTON, D.C.

J. McQueen

OPEN THE DOOR
TO A GOOD TURN

SWAYING IS ONE of the most common faults in golf. It happens when the player moves his head and body laterally to the right on the backswing. Swaying results in a loss of clubhead speed and mis-hit shots.

Normally, a golfer sways because he doesn't understand how the body should turn during the swing. He probably has heard misleading advice to "take the clubhead straight away from the ball." This causes him to shift his weight laterally

The "swayer" can be helped if he compares the golf swing to a door on a hinge. The door opens on the backswing and slams shut on the downswing.

Visualize your body as the hinge and your arms, hands and clubshaft as the door. Just as the door can't open "straight away" but must swing back on the hinge, so should the arms, hands and clubshaft swing back. Like the hinge, your body and head should remain steady (over the ball) throughout the swing.

Since your body is also slightly tilted at address a proper body turn will automatically cause the clubhead to rise on the backswing as the left lowers.

by LUCA BARBATO
PROFESSIONAL, OAKBOURNE C.C., LAFAYETTE, LA.

If your right elbow is pointing straight down at the top of the backswing, you can be sure it will properly return to the right side on the downswing.

POINT RIGHT ELBOW 'DOWN' AT TOP OF SWING

MANY GOLFERS who follow advice to keep their heads still and to stay "down" on their shots, still find themselves topping the ball or hitting it on the heel of their clubhead.

The problem often is that these golfers allow their elbow to fly away from their body on their backswing. On their downswing, their elbow fails to return to their right side. This raises the plane of the swing and produces a topped shot, or causes the clubhead to follow an outside-in path so the club's heel hits the ball.

To maintain a proper clubhead path and swing plane, the right elbow must return to the right side early on the downswing.

Check your right elbow at the top of your backswing to see that it points more or less toward the ground, instead of out and away from your body. Keeping your elbow pointed down enables you to more easily return it to your right side as you begin your downswing.

by HERB SNOW
PROFESSIONAL, KELLER GOLF CLUB, ST. PAUL, MINN.

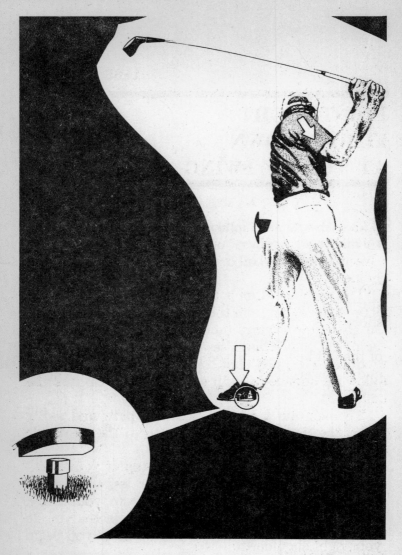

By concentrating on planting your left heel at the start of the downswing, you will encourage the shifting of your weight to your left side and the lowering of your right shoulder.

PLANT LEFT HEEL
TO START DOWNSWING

SINCE THE DOWNSWING takes place so fast, it must be started properly if a golfer is to produce successful shots.

The downswing starts with a combined lowering of the left heel, a movement of the left hip to the left, and a lowering of the right shoulder. These moves occur almost simultaneously in a well-timed swing, and any one of them will encourage the others. Thus, the wise golfer will focus his attention on making only one of these moves.

I suggest you concentrate on lowering your left heel as the "first step" in producing a well-coordinated downswing. By planting your left heel firmly, as if you were depressing a button or switch, you will automatically cause your left hip to move left and your right shoulder to lower.

by JAKE FONDREN
PROFESSIONAL, COLONIAL COUNTRY CLUB, MEMPHIS, TENN.

Women will find that if their first downswing movement is starting the rotation of their right hip counter-clockwise, their arms, hands, and club will follow in a properly timed sequence.

START DOWNSWING
WITH LOWER BODY

MANY WOMEN golfers sacrifice considerable distance on their shots by failing to realize that power should gradually build up on the downswing by means of a well-timed and orderly uncoiling of the body. Women have a tendency to rely too much on their arms to do the work on their downswing. This throws their timing off and they actually lose clubhead speed.

A critical moment for all golfers — but especially women, who need maximum power — occurs at the top of the backswing. This is where you should be conscious of holding back the arms and hands while the lower body starts uncoiling toward the target. This slight delay of the arms and hands gives you a chance to move into the downswing with proper timing. This sequence of movement — lower body first, then shoulders, arms, and hands — permits gradual acceleration of the clubhead so that, when finally the wrists begin to uncock in the hitting area, you obtain top clubhead speed when you need it most.

by CARL ROHMANN
PROFESSIONAL, LAKE VENICE GOLF CLUB, VENICE, FLA.

*The wrist cock achieved at the top of the backswing
(top) should be maintained on the downswing until
the wrists reach approximately hip level.*

START DOWNSWING
WITH WRISTS COCKED

MANY GOLFERS make the beginning of the downswing a much too complicated maneuver. The key to a good downswing is to make it as natural and uncomplicated as possible. Everything should move back toward the ball together.

"Everything," however, may be too general a term to think about. So let us consider the start of the downswing as one specific point that can easily be followed.

Presuming that the wrists have been fully cocked at the top of the backswing, the golfer then needs merely to concentrate on starting the hands straight down with the wrists still cocked.

If the wrist-cock is preserved at the start of the downswing, there will be no possibility of a "cast" from the top. This error involves uncocking the wrist too soon in the downswing, thus reducing clubhead speed and power.

In the correct swing, the wrists do not begin to uncock until they reach about hip-level on the downswing. As they uncock, clubhead speed increases.

The downswing is so fast, however, that it is a physical impossibility to consciously uncock the wrists at any one point. Merely starting down with the wrists cocked is a practically foolproof method of achieving the desired result.

by HANK BARGER
PROFESSIONAL, STARDUST COUNTRY CLUB, SAN DIEGO, CALIF.

The weight shift from the top of the swing to the start of the backswing goes from the right heel at the top (top) to the left heel as the downswing begins (bottom).

SHIFT WEIGHT HEEL-TO-HEEL DURING SWING

A KEY TO the perfectly coordinated and balanced swing is this:

A golfer should feel the bulk of his weight on his right heel at the top of his backswing, and then squarely on his left heel as soon as he starts the clubhead back to the ball.

Of course, as the clubhead is swung on through the ball, the weight gradually moves a little to the outside of the left heel.

If the right heel is firmly planted on the backswing, chances are good that the golfer has not allowed his body to sway away from the target, which would probably be the case if weight were felt on the outside of his right heel. If there is no sensation of weight on the right heel at this part of the swing, he did not properly transfer his weight in that direction equally toward both heels.

When a golfer moves his weight onto the left heel immediately as the downswing begins, he is building a properly strong left side to hit "against." The clubhead should swing past this firm left side, without any lateral sway of the upper body toward the target.

by HARRY NETTELBLADT
PROFESSIONAL, GOLF CLUB OF AVON, CONN.

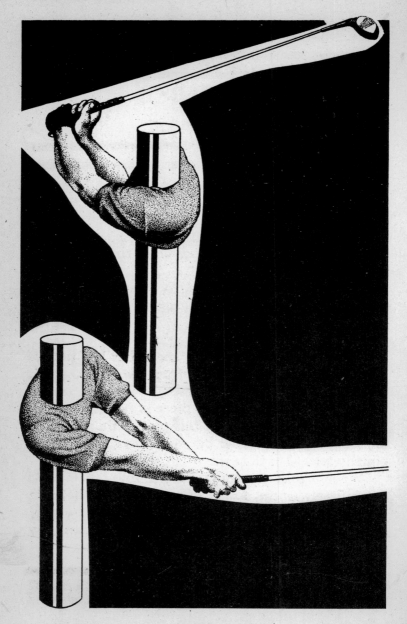

ROTATE SHOULDERS AROUND A CENTRAL POINT

FOR MAXIMUM POWER and accuracy in your golf swing, your shoulders should revolve around a central point. Imagine the upper part of your spine as being the hub or fulcrum point, which should remain in a stable position throughout your swing. Think of your spine as an axle around which your shoulders revolve (see illustrations on opposite page).

Using the upper part of your spine as the central point for your shoulders to revolve around helps keep you in good balance and provides for a full coiling of your muscles for a dynamic release of power during impact.

By revolving your shoulders around a central point, you will avoid swaying to the right on your backswing. Swaying destroys balance and disallows a full coiling of your muscles.

By the same token, revolving around the central point will prevent your upper body from moving toward the target on the downswing, which usually results in shots to the right. Your body will then properly stay behind the ball at impact.

by **LOU STRONG**
PROFESSIONAL, PGA NATIONAL GOLF CLUB

INCORRECT

CORRECT

KEEP WEIGHT 'INSIDE' RIGHT FOOT

SWAYING CREATES problems in controlling direction and achieving good distance on your shots. Swaying occurs when your body moves laterally to your right on your backswing instead of coiling or winding around a central axis.

Most often swaying causes the weight to shift to the outside of the right foot on the backswing. However, trying to correct a sway by keeping most of the weight on the left foot is not the solution. This can be equally faulty because keeping the weight to the left prevents a full hip turn and in general unnecessarily restricts your backswing.

To prevent swaying, simply make sure that ample pressure is maintained on the inside portion of your right foot on your backswing. This will help you to coil, instead of sway, your body as you swing the club back.

by JIMMY DEMARET
PROFESSIONAL, CONCORD HOTEL, KIAMESHA LAKE, N.Y.

INCORRECT

CORRECT

PULL DOWN.
SWING THROUGH

MANY GOLFERS COIL and transfer their weight properly on the backswing, but then jerk the club downward — using the hands and arms only — to start the downswing. This is called "hitting from the top," a flaw that causes pulled or sliced shots, depending on the direction that the clubface is looking during impact.

This jerky downswing eliminates the possibility of a properly smooth transfer of the weight from the right to left side. It is accompanied by a premature uncocking of the wrists, which destroys power.

To correct this problem, the golfer should feel that his shoulders and hips are turning to the left in a rhythmic motion as the downswing starts. At the same time he pulls down and through the ball with his left hand, swinging the back of this hand toward the target until well after impact.

by MORGAN BAKER
PROFESSIONAL, SHARPSTOWN C.C., HOUSTON, TEX.

INCORRECT

CORRECT

LOWER SHOULDER TO SWING CLUBHEAD ON LINE

MANY AVERAGE golfers align themselves so that they aim slightly to the right of their target. This position gives them a stronger feeling. However, on their down-swing they have a tendency to unconsciously compensate for this alignment to the right. They move their right shoulder out over the ball in order to swing the clubhead along the target line. This turning of the shoulders on a too-horizontal plane may cause the clubhead to contact the ball on an outside-in path and sliced or pulled shots often result.

Your right shoulder should move down and under your chin on your downswing so that during impact the clubhead will be moving along the target line and the clubface will be looking at the target.

By aligning slightly more to the left, then swinging his club directly at the target, a golfer will find that this proper movement of his right shoulder will occur more naturally.

by JIMMY BURKE
PROFESSIONAL, THE CHAMPIONS GOLF CLUB, HOUSTON, TEX.

By thinking of an underhanded toss of the ball toward the target, you will feel the need for maximum clubhead speed at impact to get the ball off your clubface.

'FLING' BALL TOWARD THE TARGET

TOO OFTEN, MANY average golfers destroy their timing by hitting *at* the ball instead of allowing their their clubheads to sweep *through* the hitting area. Their swing action slows down just before impact and, as a result, they produce shots that lack distance and accuracy.

I suggest that to help overcome this you first picture, in your mind's eye, the path your shot should take. Then, as you swing, imagine that the ball is attached to the face of your club. When you begin your downswing, feel that you are going to "fling" the ball off the clubface toward the target on the path that you have pictured.

Thinking of shot results before you actually hit the ball, and feeling that you are flinging the ball toward the target, will help you maintain maximum clubhead speed in the hitting area.

by BILL STRAUSBAUGH, JR.
PROFESSIONAL, TURF VALLEY COUNTRY CLUB, BALTIMORE, MD.

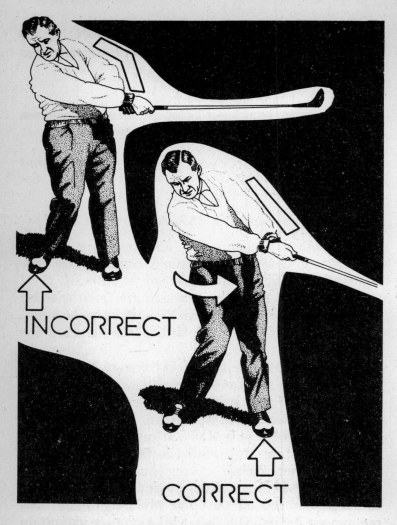

INCORRECT

CORRECT

By collapsing the left arm after impact, your weight remains mostly on your right foot causing a weak shot (top). Properly extending the left arm after impact leads your right side toward the target with your weight moving over to the left side. The result is a crisp and powerful golf shot (bottom).

LEFT ARM EXTENSION AFTER IMPACT

GOLF IS A TWO-HANDED GAME. But I have found that the left hand and arm, being weaker, must be developed to support and guide the power from the stronger right side in the correct path beyond impact.

Too many golfers physically hit at the ball and not through it. In doing so, the left side stops and the right keeps hitting. This makes for a soft, or pop, shot with very little power.

The correct position after impact finds the left arm and side extended with the left hand and arm directing the right through the ball and toward the target. Extend well beyond the ball. Then the clubhead comes up and around. The complete follow-through motion is *out*, *up* and *around*.

First practice this extension with a short iron. Once this extension in the hitting area is mastered with the shorter swing, the left arm will be in condition to continue functioning correctly in the three-quarter and full swings on long iron and wood shots.

Starting with the shorter irons will also allow you to keep your head in position while the left arm is pulling out beyond the ball. This extension definitely tends to draw the head forward with it.

by **JOE CAPELLO**
PROFESSIONAL, ARONIMINK G.C., NEWTON SQUARE, PA.

HIGH FINISH FOR
LOW SCORES

A GOOD HIGH FINISH follow-through suggests a shot
has been executed with authority and control.

To help achieve a high finish, make sure your left
wrist stays firm immediately beyond the hitting area.
When you swing your hands out toward the target,
your right arm will straighten and point toward the
target when the club becomes horizontal with the
ground. Continue this extension of your right arm as
the club moves up and around, and your hands will
finish high above your left shoulder.

Your chances of finishing high increase if you
make certain your right shoulder raises on the backswing and lowers on the downswing.

by **GEORGE BUCK**

PROFESSIONAL, EL CONQUISTADOR HOTEL & CLUB, FUJARDO, PUERTO RICO

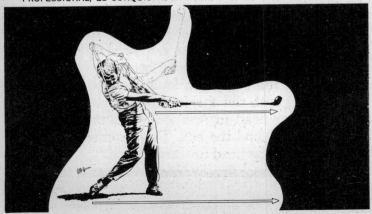

THE WOODS

The woods are your attacking clubs. If you don't hit them well, it is difficult to score on most par 4s and 5s. While you possibly can recover from weak woods play with iron shots, the odds against a low score will soar.

You don't have to "power" the ball on wood shots to gain distance. The clubs' shafts naturally lengthen the swing arc, which in turn increases clubhead speed in the impact area. While the idea is to hit the ball in the center of the clubface, off-center hits with woods often produce fairly good results.

Good woods play is especially important to women and seniors. Because they do not hit the ball as far, they will be using their woods from the fairway much more often. If they're proficient, their scores will shrink accordingly.

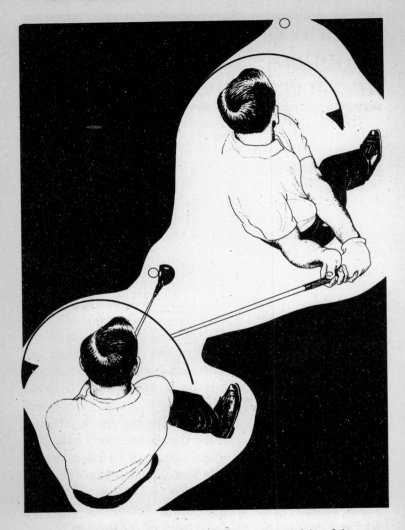

A full shoulder turn and return is essential for driving power. On the backswing your shoulders should turn in a clockwise path with no lateral movement of your body to the right (top). On the downswing, rotate your shoulders counter-clockwise to release power at impact (bottom).

A GOOD OFFENSE PRODUCES LONG AND ACCURATE DRIVES

THE ABILITY TO HIT long drives and make them carry to a specific spot will set the stage for playing a par-4 or par-5 hole in regulation. But unless your swing is well-grooved and well-timed, letting out shaft usually results in loss of balance and timing in an effort that relies too much on the arms and too little on the big back and leg muscles.

Long accurate driving comes from an "offensive" attitude. An aggressive waggle, a full shoulder turn, and perhaps a faster backswing, providing smoothness can be retained, will produce "boomers" off the tee.

In addition, here are specific tips that will add length to your drives and insure accuracy:

1. Shift your weight in the same direction that the clubhead is moving — to the right on the backswing, to the left on the downswing. But be sure that your weight never moves to the outside of your right foot.

2. Make sure that your body coils or turns on the backswing without moving laterally out of its original central-axis position.

3. Return your weight immediately to your left foot at the start of your downswing. At the same time, pull your right elbow in close to your right side.

by **HORTON SMITH**
1934, '36 MASTERS WINNER

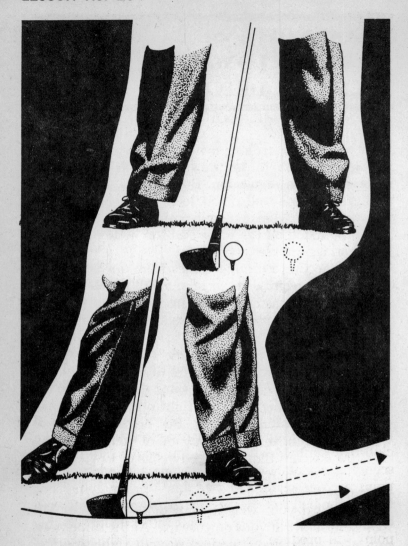

For low, boring shots into the wind, play the ball
farther back in your stance than normal (top). Impact will then occur at the bottom of your swing arc,
rather than on the upswing, giving the ball a lower
flight trajectory than normal (bottom).

CENTER THE BALL AND STRIKE IT SQUARE FOR DRIVES INTO THE WIND

WIND IS BOTHERSOME enough for the expert player, but it usually means double trouble for the average golfer who, in most cases, lacks sufficient force for his shots to "bore" into the breeze. Driving into the wind is a special problem because on such tee shots the average golfer has a tendency to "press" his swing in trying for maximum distance.

To succeed on drives into the wind, (1) play the ball a bit farther back in your stance than normal and (2) concentrate on striking the ball as squarely as possible.

Playing the ball an inch or so farther back toward the center of your stance will enable you to make club-ball contact when the clubhead is neither descending nor starting upward. Contact made at this point in your swing will give you a lower flying shot than if the ball were played farther forward and were caught on the upswing. Also, contact made at this point will produce less backspin — and thus a lower shot — than if the ball were met on the downswing.

by **CARY MIDDLECOFF**
1949, '56 U.S. OPEN WINNER

INCORRECT CORRECT

Trying to scoop the ball with a fairway wood will leave you behind the ball at impact. You probably will "top" the ball (top). By letting the club's loft do its job, you properly swing through the ball keeping your head and shoulders over the ball at impact. This insures a square clubhead-ball contact at the lowest part of the swing (bottom).

DON'T BEAT AT THE BALL WITH FAIRWAY WOODS

A GOLFER WHO BEATS the ball down the fairway, using an iron club for shots that normally would call for a wood does not feel a fairway wood has sufficient loft to put the ball in flight. This lack of trust in the club's loft could be why your fairway woods usually send the ball dribbling along the grass. You might feel you must scoop underneath the ball with fairway woods. If so, you lean back on your rear foot — away from the target and the ball — on the downswing. Altering the lowest part — or contact point — of the clubhead's arc. The clubhead touches down behind the ball, minimizing the chances for square contact.

To put fairway wood shots into the air where they belong, you first must believe that the club's loft *is* sufficient to put the ball in flight — without any scooping motion on your part.

Next you should keep your head and shoulders in the same area throughout the swing that they were in at the address position.

When this is perfected the clubhead will have a good chance of meeting the ball at the lowest point of its swing arc. The club's built-in loft will have an opportunity to do its job making the ball fly.

by PAUL HAHN
TRICK SHOT EXHIBITIONIST

Thinking of a high hand position at the top of the swing will help you put your 4-wood swing on an upright plane. This plane gives you full advantage of the club's loft at impact.

ACHIEVE A HIGH HAND POSITION FOR HIGH 4-WOOD SHOTS

THERE ARE TIMES when the high 4-wood shot can be a big stroke-saver for any golfer. When greens are hard a high 4-wood shot is ideal for shooting to the flag.

To hit the 4-wood high you should stand quite close to the ball at address. This will put your swing on an upright plane so that you can take full advantage of the club's loft at impact.

After the clubhead goes straight back from the ball for two or three inches, it should begin its move upward. Aided by a full turn of the shoulders, your hands should move to a high position above your shoulders, even higher than they would be on a drive.

This high hand position is important because the high 4-wood should be played more like a 3- or 4-iron than a driver. The club should move into the ball more at a downward angle than it does on the drive, when it sweeps the ball into flight.

High hands on the backswing put you in proper position to pull the club almost sharply downward into the ball. Remember that the 4-wood has considerable loft — usually about 20 degrees. Do not try to scoop or sweep the ball into flight.

by **BYRON NELSON**
1937, '42 MASTERS WINNER

71

INCORRECT

CORRECT

An abrupt takeaway with the driver usually leaves too much weight on the left foot and the wrists cock too soon (top). By taking the club away from the ball low and slow, you give your body a chance to properly shift its weight to the right side helping your wrists to cock at the right time and your hips tilt and turn (bottom).

START THE DRIVER BACK LOW

ONE WAY TO HELP yourself drive successfully is to stress a low takeaway of the clubhead when starting the backswing. Take it back close to the ground for at least eight inches.

The club should go back in a wide arc on all wood and long iron shots, but especially the drives because on those shots the ball is being "swept" off the tee rather than hit with a downward moving clubhead. You want approximately the same sweeping motion on your takeaway as you will have in the hitting area.

Taking the club back in a nice wide arc will not only lengthen your swing but also assure a low takeaway.

Another reason for taking the club back low is to prevent premature cocking of the wrists, and resultant loss of power and club control that occurs when the club is lifted too abruptly.

One word of caution: when executing the low takeaway be sure that your weight shifts to the inside of the right foot on the backswing and not beyond to the outside. Keeping the weight on the inside will encourage a tilting and turning of the body rather than a lateral swaying to the right.

by SAM PENECALE

PROFESSIONAL, WHITEMARSH VALLEY C.C., PHILADEPHIA, PA.

THE LONG IRONS

There are precious few holes where an iron shot is not needed. About the only exception for you would be par-3s where it takes a wood off the tee to reach the green. But even in these cases you'll probably miss the green often — and need an iron to get the ball onto the putting surface.

Irons are the golfer's accuracy weapons, the clubs that get the ball into decent putting range on the green. If you're proficient with them you will get your share of one-putt greens.

Being able to play your long irons well is essential to low golf scores. If you have confidence in your long irons, you will have little problem with the rest of your clubs. Being able to hit the ball with the long shafts and small clubfaces with reduced loft of the long irons will make middle and short iron shots much easier. Also, when accuracy outweighs distance off the tee or on the fairway, such as on a fairly long hole with an extremely tight fairway, the good long iron swinger will keep his shot in play without sacrificing much distance.

HUM AWAY THOSE LONG IRON BLUES

GOLFERS WITH perfectly good swings often are unsuccessful with the less-lofted long irons because they think they must help the ball into the air. Actually the same rhythmical swing which produces good shots for them with other clubs is also essential to their long iron play. They should emphasize making the backswing with a good pivot and a full extension of the arms.

What might help you remember the similarity in swing rhythm between the long irons and other clubs, is humming the same tune while practicing short irons and long irons. Then you know your basic swing rhythm is working for you when you use all your clubs.

by EDDIE THOMPSON
PROFESSIONAL, SEA ISLAND GOLF CLUB, SEA ISLAND, GA.

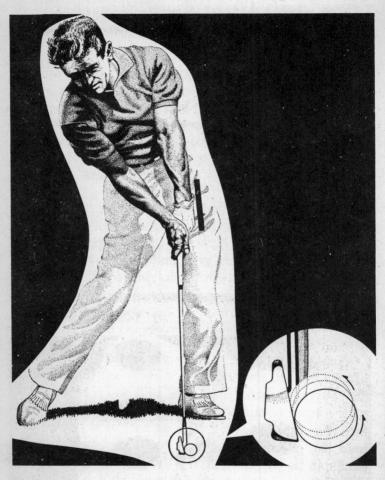

The key to success with long irons is to make sure you contact the ball before hitting the turf. This will give you the backspin you need for long-iron accuracy (inset). To achieve this, make sure you keep your wrists firm at impact.

CONTACT BALL FIRST WITH LONG IRONS

I SOMETIMES THINK amateur players shy away from hitting the long irons for fear the ball will roll over the green. They fail to realize that a good green will hold a properly executed 2- or 3-iron shot almost as well as it will an 8- or 9-iron.

Many amateur players try to lift the ball with the long iron, hoping to get more loft on the shot. They use too much hand action and try to scoop the ball into the air. Their left wrist collapses during impact and they hit the shot fat (behind the ball), or scuff or top it.

You should hit the ball first with the long irons just as you do the short ones. Keeping the left wrist firm beyond impact, strike the ball and then graze the turf in front of the ball. The ball will roll up the club-face during impact and take on sufficient backspin to hold the green. A long iron will carry just as much backspin as the short iron if hit in this manner. The short iron will stop a little quicker, but only because the club lifts it on a higher trajectory.

by PAUL HARNEY
PROFESSIONAL, PLEASANT VALLEY C.C., SUTTON, MASS.

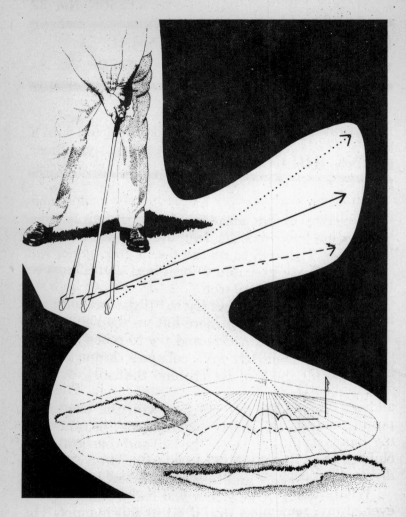

How far the ball will roll once it hits the green is determined by its position in my stance. If I play the ball well forward in my stance, the ball will stop quickly (dotted lines); if its slightly forward in my stance, it will roll a little more (solid lines); and if it's in the center of my stance, it will roll even more (broken lines).

FINESSING LONG IRONS WILL SAVE STROKES

MANY TIMES just getting the ball on the green with a long iron isn't good enough. On large greens you must finish consistently close to the hole, or you may three-putt. This means a "finesse" shot.

The 3-iron is the club I usually rely on for long iron "finesse" shots. You have to determine beforehand if the shot calls for a low or high trapectory, or a fadeaway, or a cut shot.

If I've got a shot of 3-iron distance, but I know that the green is hard, I want to hit the shot high so it won't bounce over. I'll play the ball farther forward in my stance than normal about opposite my left heel. Then I'll give it a lot of wrist action at impact so the clubhead catches up with my hands and sweeps the ball away. The shot will fly high and stop quickly.

Frequently I need a low boring 3-iron. Then I address the ball farther back than normal, about opposite stance center. I move into the ball firmly with my hands leading the clubhead and try to keep the clubhead low to the ground well beyond impact. The divot will appear ahead of the original ball position.

Whatever type of 3-iron shot you plan to use, however, always remember two basic fundamentals: First, grip firmly with both hands. Second, take a long smooth swing with a wide arc.

by SAM SNEAD
1949, '52, '54 MASTERS WINNER

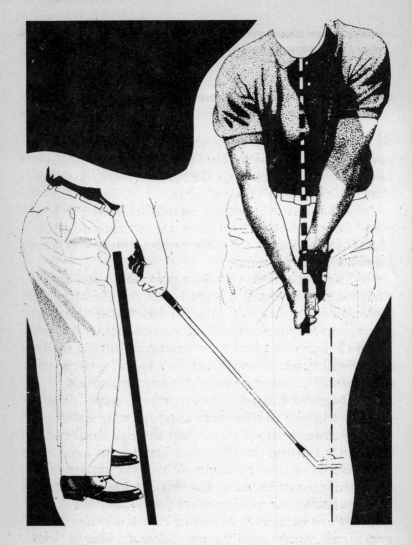

For a 2-iron fade, rotate your grip so the Vs formed by your thumbs and forefingers point to your chin (top) and your stance is open with your left foot pulled away from the intended line of flight (bottom).

FADE WITH A 2-IRON FOR CONTROL

MANY AVERAGE GOLFERS find a 2-iron a difficult club to control because of its small club face and low loft. But I believe that the 2-iron can become an effective long iron for you if you learn how to fade the ball with it.

A 2-iron fade will cause the ball to fly from left to right in the air. When the ball does hit the turf it will not roll as far as it would on a normal 2-iron shot. On approach shots, if the ball lands on or close to the green, it will stay near where it initially lands.

The key to a 2-iron fade is the grip. In a normal grip, you should be able to see two or three knuckles of your left hand at address. For the 2-iron fade, rotate your grip to the left so that only one knuckle of your left hand is showing. The Vs formed by your thumbs and forefingers will point almost to your chin rather than over your right shoulder. Do not open the face of the club.

Line up your feet so you are facing slightly to the left of the intended target. Your ball is going to travel from left-to-right. Finally, position your feet so that the ball is forward in your stance and your hands are over the ball at address. Now your all set for a controlled long-iron shot that will produce results.

by **JIMMY DEMARET**
PROFESSIONAL, CONCORD HOTEL, KIAMESHA LAKE, N.Y.

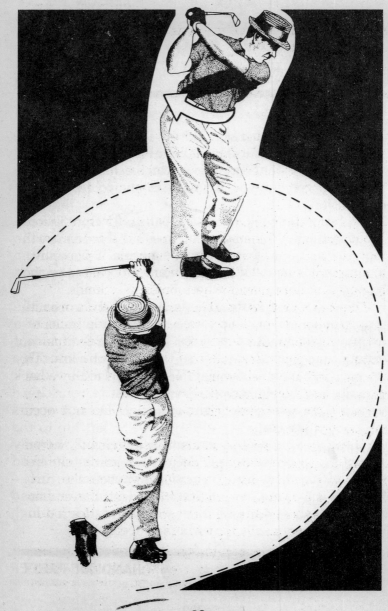

MIDDLE IRON SHOTS NEED A FULL BODY TURN AND HIGH FINISH

MIDDLE IRONS ARE often the clubs you need for approach shots on medium-length par-4s.

I feel that there are two key points to consider when hitting these clubs. First, make sure that you take a rather full body turn on the backswing. Second, complete your swing so that the hands are high at the finish. By incorporating this advice you will avoid the short jerky stroke that often destroys timing on iron shots.

To make a full turn, you should feel that on the backswing the club moves back and up because of a tilting and turning of the shoulders and hips, not solely because of moving the hands and arms. This turning of the form causes the clubhead to move back slightly inside the imaginary target line.

The high finish will be ineffective unless it occurs as a natural result of fully turning the left hip to the left on the downswing. This "left side lead" not only clears a path for the hands and brings the clubhead downward — first into the ball and then the turf — but it also forces the hands to thrust the clubhead toward the target and then up into the desired high finish.

by CHANDLER HARPER
1950 PGA WINNER

THE SHORT IRONS
AND APPROACH SHOTS

Short irons are your "last-ditch" clubs. If you have executed your other shots properly, one more good one with a short iron can bring your ball within possible one-putt distance of the hole, and that could mean a birdie.

Also, if things haven't gone well before it's time to use them, talented accuracy with your short irons can make up for mistakes.

Most teaching professionals feel that the short irons are the easiest clubs to learn to use effectively. They have shorter shafts, which require a shorter and, therefore, mor econtrollable swing. Their high angle of clubface loft makes it simpler to get the ball airborne. The clubfaces are, too, larger than those of the irons. There's more surface on which to hit the ball. Learning the lessons presented in this section will develop skill in the "scoring" area of your game. You'll count on these shots time and again on the course.

EXECUTE APPROACH SHOTS WITH AUTHORITY

THE DECISION of whether to play an approach shot to carry onto, or short of, a green occurs frequently in golf, especially for those who play on courses with unusually firm greens.

Once you decide which type of shot to play, execute the shot with a firm resolve. Don't try to "wish" the ball onto the green. A firm, crisp stroke is especially vital if you play your approach to carry the green. These shots require a maximum amount of backspin if they are to come to rest quickly on the putting surface.

Such backspin is best achieved by an accelerating clubhead that strikes down on the ball before cutting into the turf. Imagine that you are going to slice through the ball from 3 o'clock to 7 o'clock (see illustration below). Make sure that your wrists are firm as they lead the clubhead through the hitting area.

by TEX McCHAREN

PROFESSIONAL, SHERWOOD FOREST COUNTRY CLUB, BATON ROUGE, LA.

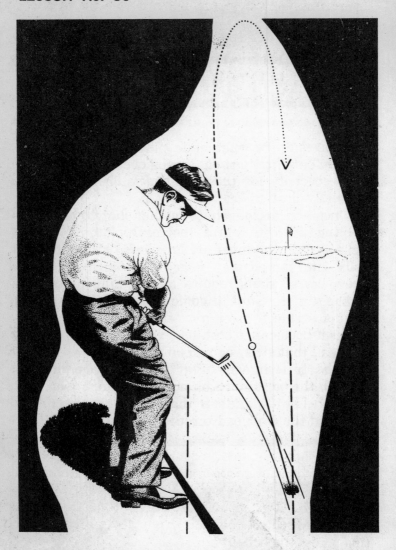

For a cut shot, open your stance and lay back your clubface at address. The open stance makes my downswing take an outside-in arc so that the clubface cuts across the ball.

USE A CUT SHOT FOR
A MIDDLE-IRON FINESSE

A FINESSE SHOT to small greens can often make the difference between par and bogey for the average golfer.

The ideal finesse shot to small greens finds the ball carrying a great deal of backspin, but still flying high, so that it drops softly, more or less straight down, onto the green.

However, when I face a middle iron finesse shot requiring more "stop" than normal, I try to hit a high, soft "cut" shot. I open my stance slightly so that my right foot is closer to the target line than my left. At address I open the clubface very slightly so that it faces just a hair to the right. This open face increases the loft of the club just enough to assure a high shot. My open stance enables me to bring the clubhead into the ball slightly from the outside so that I cut across the ball. The glancing blow that results produces a shot that settles gently on the green.

This cut shot will not go as far as a normal shot with the iron in question, so I'd advise using one less-lofted club. Also aim the shot a bit to the left of target to allow for the slight fade that will result from cutting across the ball.

by JACK FLECK
1955 U.S. OPEN WINNER

LEAD WITH YOUR LEFT SIDE TO 'BITE' WITH YOUR WEDGE

Backspin plays an important role when you are faced with short pitch shots requiring "bite." The illustrations below show how backspin is applied to the ball.

The leading edge of the clubhead strikes the ball as the club is still moving downward slightly compressing the ball, which backspins up the clubface. Finally the ball rebounds off the clubface, still backspinning, as the clubhead cuts into the turf well ahead of the ball's original position.

The backspinning should be short with an early and definite wrist cock. The left side should lead the downswing, turning out of the way to give room for the left hand to pull the club down and through the ball. An open stance, with the left foot pulled back, will help you turn your left side clear on the downswing.

by **BYRON NELSON**
1937, '42 MASTERS WINNER

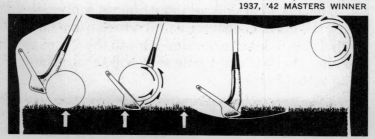

BOUNCE BALL ONTO ELEVATED GREEN

PLAYING A SHORT shot to an 'elevated green often requires the ball to stop near the hole without running way past. Many times a "bank-climbing" shot, where the ball bounces up the incline, onto the green and comes to rest after just a little roll, will do the job.

Use a club with little loft, like the 2-iron. Play the ball to and intially just short of the bank. You want the ball to take low, running bounces rather than large bounces which are apt to make it die.

Position the ball back in your stare, possibly even right of center. Hit sharply downward on the ball. You'll obtain better results of you choke down a bit on the club.

by CHARLES HOFFNER
PROFESSIONAL, DELRAY BEACH (FLA.) COUNTRY CLUB.

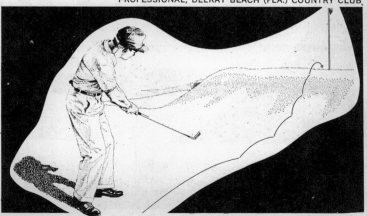

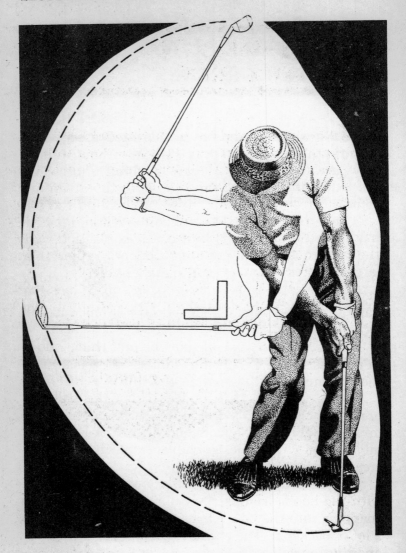

For a lob shot, play the ball to the front of your stance, break your wrists early in the backswing, and use a very upright swing plane. This will result in a high shot with plenty of backspin.

INCREASE YOUR LOFT
FOR LOB SHOTS

WHEN I'M PITCHING over a hazard or a mound and have little green between me and the hole, I try to hit a high, soft "lob" shot, usually with my pitching wedge but occasionally even with the sand wedge. I want a shot that will fly high and slow — one that will settle in its tracks.

To execute this type of shot the first thing I do is to address the ball with the clubface laid back more than normal, thus increasing the loft.

I take the club straight back from the ball and break my wrists early in the backswing. This gives my swing an upright plane and assures that I won't hit the ball with a closed clubface, which would decrease the loft.

On the return stroke I strike down and through with the hands leading the clubhead, and the wrists snapping into the ball. This gives me a high lob with a lot of backspin. The entire swing should be leisurely and rhythmical.

by **SAM SNEAD**
1949, '52, '54 MASTERS WINNER

CHIP SHOT FORMULA:
1/3 BY AIR, 2/3 BY LAND

THE SECRET TO chipping your ball up to the hole consistently is not merely having a "feel" for the shot. You must also have a logical never-varying method for gauging your shot and for selecting your club.

Using the Nos. 4, 5, 6 and 7 irons as your basic chipping arsenal, you can develop a method for measuring your needs on every short chip shot by dividing the distance from your ball to the hole into imaginary thirds. Your goal on all short chips should be to send the ball one-third of the distance in the air, and the remaining two-thirds along the surface of the green. By practicing with each of your four chipping irons, you quickly will understand the capabilities of each club.

by **ERNIE VOSSLER**
PROFESSIONAL, QUAIL CREEK COUNTRY CLUB, OKLAHOMA CITY, OKLA.

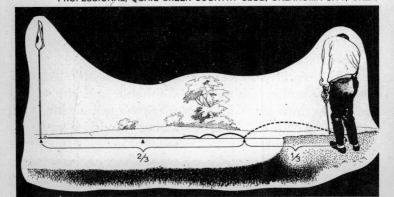

IMAGINE YOU'RE TOSSING THE BALL ONTO THE GREEN WHEN CHIPPING

THERE ARE SEVERAL ways to judge the force needed on a given chip shot. Some feel you should note the overall distance and let the ball land where it may. More proficient players seem to prefer hitting to a landing spot on the green and letting the roll take care of itself.

One of the best aids is to imagine how a ball would react if you tossed it by hand toward the cup. Simulate an underhand toss of the ball onto the green. Then transfer this movement to the proper chip shot technique. This is the best way to attune your muscles. Judging a chip will soon become merely a matter of using your imagination.

by JACK BURKE
1956 MASTERS WINNER

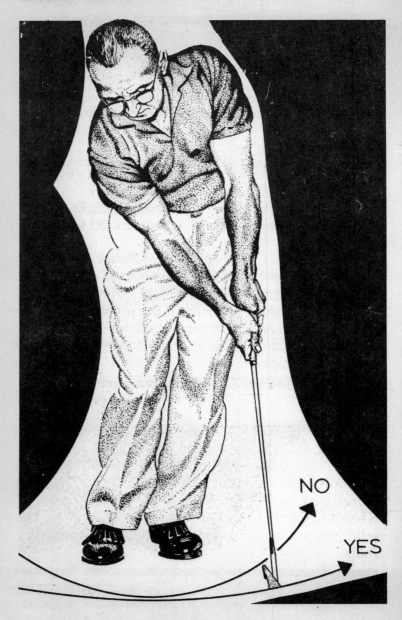

NO

YES

FIRM WRISTS FOR SOLID CHIPS

THE CHIP SHOT can be a great stroke-saver but it often gives considerable trouble to players who are too "wristy" in making the stroke.

Lifting the club abruptly on the backswing and snapping the wrists on the downstroke turns the desired crisp stroke into an ineffective scooping motion. A scooped swing often takes turf before the club meets the ball and thus fails to send the ball the intended distance. The scooping motion also can lead to "skulling" the shot (hitting the ball on the upswing) and sending it scooting far past the hole.

The correct chipping stroke has a minimum of wrist break. The arms and hands take the club back low to the ground. The left arm and hand lead the clubhead down and through the ball on the downstroke. The normal loft of the clubface will produce the desired flight and amount of roll if the left hand moves past the ball without the left wrist breaking. Keep wrist action to a minimum and you will get the solid, crisp contact needed for consistency on chip shots.

by BRUCE HERD
1963 PGA TEACHING PROFESSIONAL OF THE YEAR

PUTTING

More golf instruction has been written about putting than any other stroke. Maybe that's natural, because putting is the most exasperating part of the game. Many a score has been ruined by a missed short putt. On the other hand, what is more thrilling than a long "snake' that finds the bottom of the cup?

Putting is the most individualistic of golf shots. A bewildering variety of stances, swings and even grips can be observed on the professional tour as well as at any club. There is no way to say which is best. The flippy-wrist style of Julius Boros can work just as well as the iron-handed technique of Arnold Palmer.

The following lessons apply to all styles. No matter how you putt, you'll find the advice pertinent.

ACCELERATE PUTTING STROKE TO GET THE BALL TO THE HOLE

THERE IS ONE RULE that all good players try to follow on the green: Never leave a putt short of the hole.

Getting the ball to the hole largely depends on the type of stroke taken.

To do this accelerate your stroke into the ball. A short crisp movement will help keep your putts from falling short of the hole, or below it in the case of sidehillers. Try to hit the ball flush in the middle of the putter blade, or on the center of your putter's balance. Imagine that you are hammering a tack into a board. The follow-through should be rather abrupt. The wrists should be comparatively stiff at the finish, especially on shorter putts.

by BOBBY HILL
PROFESSIONAL, CRAIG HILL C.C., BROCKPORT, N.Y.

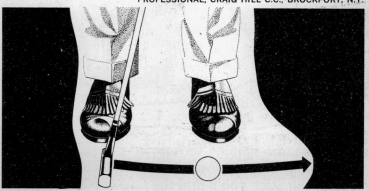

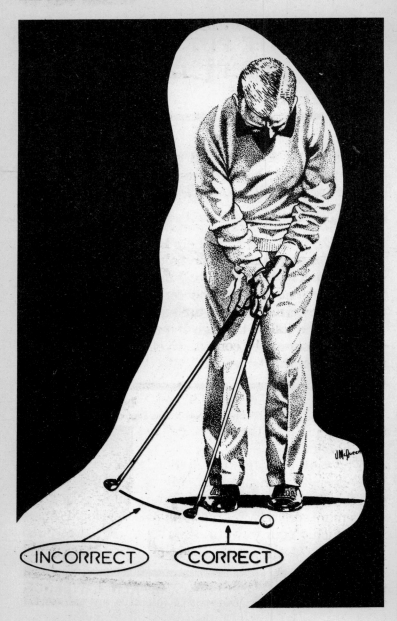

INCORRECT   CORRECT

FIRM STROKE
FOR LONG PUTTS

THE MOST COMMON FAULT of the average golfer on long putts is leaving the ball too short of, or too far past, the hole. Improper distance causes more three-putt greens than does improper direction.

Failure to stroke the ball a proper distance is often blamed on bad "touch" or lack of "feel." Actually, two mechanical faults contribute as much, if not more, to the problem.

Moving the head during the stroke encourages topped or scuffed putts. A long backswing may have the same effect if the player eases into the ball with "dead" hands.

The better putters use a short, crisp stroke, and they keep their head as steady as possible. If you practice this technique, you will not only strike your putts more squarely, but you will also develop a sensitive touch. Your reward will be fewer three-putt greens.

by KEN LAWRENCE
PROFESSIONAL, LAKEWOOD COUNTRY CLUB, NEW ORLEANS, LA.

VISUALIZE WIDE-PATH PUTTING LINE

TOO OFTEN WHEN addressing a putt, the golfer imagines a thin line extending from ball to cup. He, psychologically, has an extremely narrow target.

The target is a cup 4¼-inch diameter. The golfer should visualize not a line but a channel as wide as the hole running from cup to ball. Of course the ball must still roll truly on line to drop in the hole, but if the golfer has pictured the broad channel or track instead of the narrow line, he is apt to execute his putt in a more relaxed and confident frame of mind.

by **ERNIE EDWARDS**
PROFESSIONAL, STARMOUNT FOREST COUNTRY CLUB, GREENSBORO, N.C.

IMAGINE PUTTING TO SQUARE HOLE

IF YOU'RE having trouble dropping your putts into the circular hole, try stroking them into an imaginary "square" that measures 4¼ inches on each side — the exact diameter of the actual cup. This square has a 4¼-inch opening facing any side from which the ball may approach the cup.

For a sidehill putt from the right, there's a 4¼-inch opening on that side. The same goes for the other side.

Thinking of the cup as a 4¼-inch square offers the mental picture that there is more entry room for the ball than there appears to be when you aim for the curved front segment of the circular cup.

That square gives you 4-to-1 odds of sinking the putt and those are pretty good odds.

by **CHARLES TEEL**
PROFESSIONAL, PARADISE VALLEY C.C., LAS VAGES, NEV.

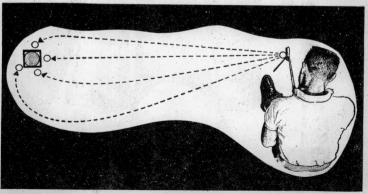

PLAY BALL FORWARD
FOR SMOOTH PUTTING

MANY GOLFERS who manage successful shots from the tee and fairway sometimes disregard one important fundamental when they arrive at the green. They often play the ball too far back in their stance on putts. As a result, their putter contacts the ball on the downstroke. The ball bounces and rolls off line.

When your putterface contacts the ball it should be square and low to the ground so that the putt rolls smoothly along the intended line.

Play the ball opposite your left toe and keep your eyes over the ball. Then your putter will contact the ball at the lowest point of its arc and help insure a putt that will roll smoothly.

by DAVE CAROLAN
PROFESSIONAL, UPPER MONTCLAIR (N.J.) COUNTRY CLUB

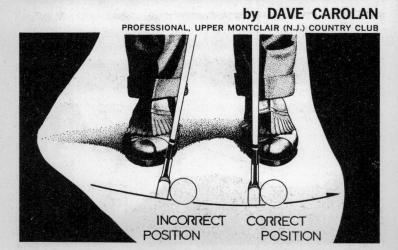

INCORRECT POSITION   CORRECT POSITION

USE PUTTER
FROM FRINGE

MANY GOLFERS FEEL that putting from the fringe is "amateurish." Nothing could be farther from the truth.

Better players realize they have less control with a lofted iron than they do with a putter. The putt is the easiest shot in golf to stroke squarely. Even from the fringe, the ball will roll to the hole without backspin.

When using the putter as a "Texas wedge", stroke the ball at bit more firmly than normal to get it through the longer fringe grass. Keep your left wrist firm throughout the stroke.

Do not use a "Texas wedge" unless your ball sits high enough for the clubface to strike it unimpeded by intervening blades of grass. Also, never use the putter when the grass lies against the line of your shot. (See illustrations below.)

by CAM PUGET
PROFESSIONAL, PEBBLE BEACH (CALIF.) COUNTRY CLUB

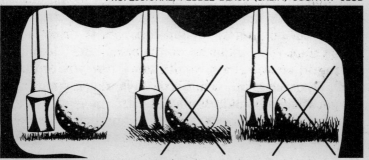

TROUBLE SHOTS

A mark of all successful golfers is that they do not give up in the face of adversity. When they shoot into trouble, they take the time to analyze the situation and find the best way to play the next shot.

Frustrating as it may be, this is one of the most fascinating parts of the game. If you never had to contend with difficult shots, much of the challenge would be eliminated. What fun would there be if every shot were taken from a "normal" lie? Or to put it the other way, how would you know you're doing well, if, on occasion, you didn't have to use your brain to get the ball back into play?

You should expect a certain number of trouble shots in every round. Walter Hagen used to say this, and when he bumped into them he wasn't disappointed. He accepted them as part of the game and didn't grouse inwardly — or outwardly — about how he got there. He went ahead and made the best of the situation. This is an attitude all golfers should take(although admittedly there are times when it would seem that the "gods of golf" are against you).

In general, it is wise to take the shortest route back into play when one of your shots goes off-line. The golfer who takes unnecessary risks from "tiger country" will usually compound his problems.

There will be times, of course, when you'll need a bold shot — when you have no other choice for salvaging a decent score on a hole. Then you have to go for broke. If the shot comes off it will be doubly advantageous; it sets you up for a good score on the hole, and it confounds opponents who thought they had you in the bag.

The lessons in this section cover many situations. If you're a serious golfer you will read them all, and then actually *practice* the shots. It doesn't do a lot of good to know theory behind the techniques unless you practice them. If trouble shots are practiced, you'll have that extra grain of confidence when you run into them in competition. Too many golfers practice only the shots they know best, and/or the ones they'll encounter if they make no bad swings.

Despite practice, there are bound to be times when a new and unexpected situation will come up. Then you must improvise. You might want to bounce the ball off a tree, or hit it backwards between your legs. The overriding point is — stick in there. Many a miraculous victory has been achieved by golfers who appeared to be hopelessly beaten.

When hitting from hard pan or sparse turf, concentrate on bringing the face of the club directly into the back of the ball without contacting the ground before impact.

STAY LOOSE WHEN LIE IS TIGHT

A "TIGHT" LIE, in which the ball nestles into grass or otherwise rests on bare ground, need not hurt your score on a hole, especially if you remain unawed by the situation.

The best advice on such a shot is merely to concentrate on making solid contact with the ball. Club selection and swing need not be altered, unless the ball is in deep rough or a divot hole. Just relax and swing easy for maximum balance and club control. Don't make a special project out of the problem. Figure that since no one expects you to succeed from such a lie, you have everything to gain.

Tight lies come in two types: grassy, and hardpan or sparse turf. A ball hit from a grassy lie will tend to fly and roll a little farther than normal. In either case, merely imagine how you will slide the clubface downward along the back of the ball during impact.

This extra effort to make good contact, despite an unfavorable lie, often produces a better-than-normal swing, and a better-than-expected shot.

by AL WATROUS
RETIRED PROFESSIONAL, OAKLAND HILLS C.C., BIRMINGHAM, MICH.

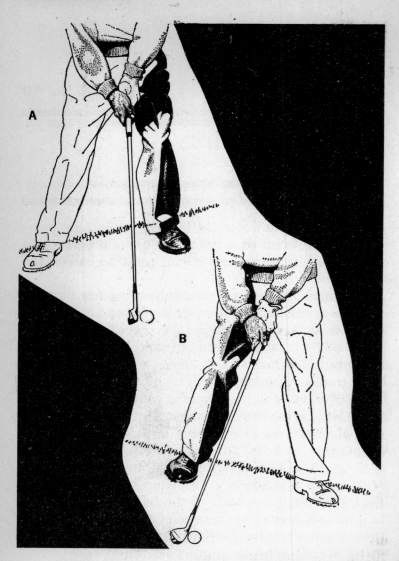

On uphill lies, play the ball forward in your stance (top). On downhill lies, play it back in your stance (bottom).

ON HILLY LIES
HIT FROM
'HIGH' FOOT

UPHILL AND DOWNHILL lies needn't be a problem to a golfer if he simply remembers to "play the ball off the 'high' foot."

Because of the terrain, when playing from an uphill lie, your clubhead reaches the ground a bit later in the swing — so you should position the ball toward your left foot. On a downhill lie the clubhead reaches the ground earlier in the swing — so play the ball back toward your right foot.

It also helps to keep most of your weight on the "high side" at the start of the swing. This offsets the normal gravitational pull toward the lower foot which causes the tendency to hook from an uphill lie and slice from a downhill lie.

Remember that you get a higher and shorter flight from an uphill lie, so use a less lofted club than usual — a 4- or 5-iron where you would normally hit a 6-iron. Hitting from a downhill slope produces a lower flight, so be sure to use a more lofted club.

by HARDY LOUDERMILK
PROFESSIONAL, OAK HILLS COUNTRY CLUB, SAN ANTONIO, TEX.

When you're above the ball on a hill, lean back with your weight on your heels (top). When your below the ball, keep your weight more toward your toes (bottom).

'CHAIN YOURSELF TO THE HILL'

WHEN A GOLFER HITS a poor shot from a sidehill lie it is often because the force of gravity pulled him off balance while he was swinging.

To lick this natural tendency to "fall down the hill," chain yourself to the slope. Of course, you can't use a chain, but you *can* remember to keep your weight back on your heels when you're standing above the ball and toward your toes when your feet are below the ball.

Swinging easier than normal also will help you retain your balance. To compensate for the distance you'll lose, take a longer club — for example, a 4- or 5-iron instead of a 6-iron. The longer club will help you reach the ball when it's below your feet, but you'll have to grip down on the shaft when it's above your feet because the ball will be closer to your hands.

by PHIL PERKINS
PROFESSIONAL, HIGHLAND PARK GOLF COURSE, CLEVELAND, O.

HOOD CLUBFACE FOR EXPLOSION FROM BURIED LIE

WHEN YOUR BALL is buried in dry, loose sand where only the top of the ball can be seen, a strong explosion shot is needed to get out.

Plant your feet firmly in the sand with the ball positioned slightly to the right of center in your stance — a bit farther back than for a normal sand shot. Hood the face of the club so it will dig into the sand about an inch or two behind the ball. Use a full power stroke with your head still and your eyes fixed to the spot where the clubhead will enter the sand, and follow through so that the clubhead will pass under the ball. The sand will force the ball out.

by JOE LOPEZ, SR.
PGA TEACHING PROFESSIONAL

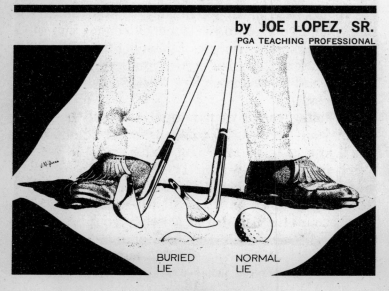

BURIED
LIE

NORMAL
LIE

PLAY SIDEHILL SHOTS TO CURVE WITH SLOPE

O<small>N</small> <small>SIDEHILL SHOTS</small>, change your aim, not your swing. The ball will usually travel in the same direction that the hill slopes. When the ball is above your feet, it will tend to fly to the left; when it is below your feet, it will tend to fly to the right.

Compensate for this tendency by aiming slightly to the right when the hill slopes left, and by aiming to the left when the hill slopes right.

by EARL STEWART, JR.
PROFESSIONAL, OAK CLIFF COUNTRY CLUB, DALLAS, TEX.

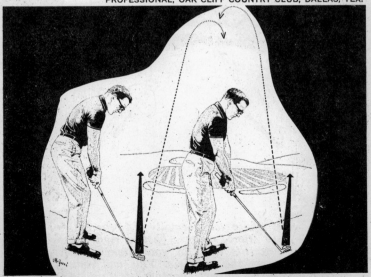

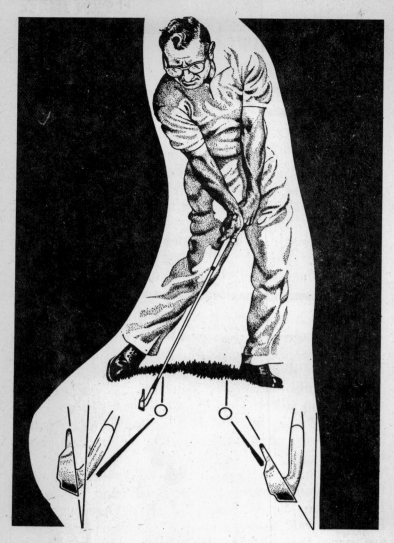

For a shot where you normally play the ball to the left of your stance center (bottom right), move it back toward the right of your stance when you want to keep the ball low. This will reduce the clubface loft at impact (bottom left).

HOW TO HIT 'WIND CHEATERS'

When a stiff wind blows, golf scores tend to rise higher than normal. The only way to keep your scores from becoming inflated by the breeze is to hit your shots lower than normal. Here are two things you can do to keep your shots down low where the wind has a minimum effect:

1. Take a less-lofted club (for example, a 4- or a 5-iron for what normally would be a 6-iron shot) and restrict your swing to about three-quarter length. The less-lofted club produces a lower flight and so does the shorter swing — it generates less clubhead speed, which is one of the things that sends a ball high in the air.

2. For all shots except the driver, play the ball a little to the right of the center of your stance. This automatically will make you lift the club more abruptly on the backswing and return it in a sharp descent striking the ball with reduced clubface loft. This clubface angle sends the ball drilling low into the wind.

Growing up in Texas, where the breeze is a big factor in golf, I watched some great wind player — Ben Hogan, Byron Nelson, Jimmy Demaret and Billy Maxwell, to name four. When wind conditions are severe they all keep the ball low, and that leads to low scores.

by ERNIE VOSSLER
PROFESSIONAL, QUAIL CREEK GOLF AND COUNTRY CLUB

To escape from rough, play the ball to the right of your stance to keep your swing arc upright. This will help your club to come right down on the ball minimizing the amount of intervening grass at impact (inset).

WHEN IN ROUGH
THINK FIRST OF ESCAPE

WHEN I FIND my ball in rough, my first thought — and it should be yours, too — is to make sure that my next shot puts me into a favorable position, even if it means sacrificing distance. Your first goal should always be to escape. Don't leave it in the rough or carelessly play into other difficulty.

Club selection is an important point to remember when escaping from rough. Unless the rough is extremely long or your ball has settled deep into the grass, you may find that your ball will actually fly and roll farther than normal, because grass that wedges between the clubface and the ball minimizes backspin. Therefore, always consider the possible necessity of using a more-lofted club.

The objects of the swing itself are (1) to contact the ball as squarely as possible; (2) to minimize the amount of grass between your club and the ball, and (3) to swing through the grass with a minimum loss of clubhead speed.

To achieve square contact, focus attention on the back of the ball and keep your head as still as possible during the swing.

To minimize the amount of intervening grass, use a more upright swing than normal with more weight than normal on the left foot throughout the swing.

by DOW FINSTERWALD
1958 PGA WINNER

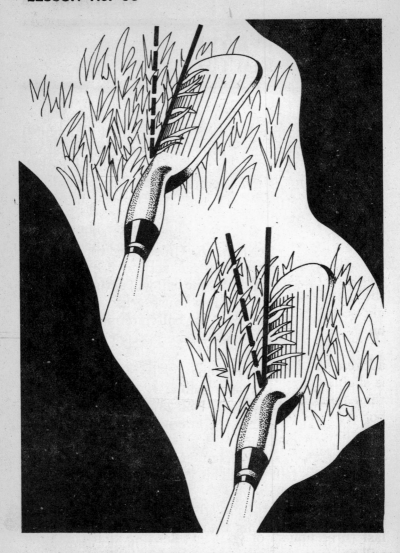

(Top) The high grass in rough will cause your club face to open at impact. (Bottom) By closing your clubface slightly at address (dotted line), it will be right on line with the target at impact.

CLOSE CLUBFACE
WHEN IN ROUGH

I FIND THAT MANY PLAYERS make the mistake on shots from rough of opening the clubface so that it looks to the right of target at the address position. They do this because the open face increases the club's loft. Players seem to feel that they need this additional lift to make the ball clear the deep grass.

Unfortunately an open clubface on shots from rough only compounds a problem that is inherent with such shots. This problem is the tendency of grass encountered by the clubhead on the downswing to open the clubface slightly just before impact. This opening occurs because the grass exerts its greatest drag on the toe end of the club.

To compensate for this drag I suggest that golfers address the ball on these shots with a clubface that is slightly closed — looking to left of target — rather than open. Don't worry about getting the ball airborne from the rough. It will climb right up the clubface and take off at the normal angle you would expect from the club in hand.

The grass drag you encounter on shots from rough also will be minimized if you (1) employ an upright swing to cut down on the amount of grass your clubhead must encounter and (2) grip firmly with the last three fingers of your left hand so that this drag will not turn the club.

by **GRAHAM ROSS**
PROFESSIONAL, DALLAS ATHLETIC CUB C.C., DALLAS, TEX.

'BLAST' FROM FLUFFY ROUGH

ON PROFESSIONAL TOUR COURSES, especially those prepared for major championships, the grass is often allowed to grow long around the fringe of the green. It
becomes very light and fluffy and the ball sinks into
the grass.

Ordinarily, being this close to the green would
call for a long-rolling chip shot, but such a shot is impossible from the long grass. You cannot hood a six
or seven iron and execute this shot with any consistency. The thick grass will usually slow down the club
so much that the ball will not travel the distance
desired. Or you will strike the ball firmly to overcome
the rough's resistance and the shot will roll far past
the hole.

I recommend you play this shot with a wedge and
imagine you are blasting from sand. Position the ball
forward, opposite your left foot, and open your stance
by drawing the left foot away from the target line.
This puts the clubhead in front of the hands at address and increases its effective loft.

Swing the clubhead into the grass about an inch
or so behind the ball. The wedge's wide flange allows
the clubhead to ride through the grass under the ball,
giving it a high trajectory to land on the green softly
with very little roll. Use enough power to carry the
ball close to the pin and you'll recover for more pars.

by JULIUS BOROS
PROFESSIONAL, MID-PINES CLUB, SOUTHERN PINES, N.C.

CORRECT

INCORRECT

LEAD WITH YOUR HANDS WHEN LIE IS TIGHT

I FIND THAT MANY amateur golfers become alarmed and lose confidence when they find they must play a shot from hard-baked ground with little or no grass cushioning the ball.

On such occasions, many players feel they must scoop the ball to make it fly. They allow their hands to lag behind the clubhead as it moves into the ball. The usual result is either a scuffed or a topped shot.

You should realize that your clubs are built to loft the ball into flight, even from such tight lies. All you must do is implement the manufacturer's design with a proper swing.

If you strike the ball with a sharply descending blow and with your hands leading the clubhead (see illustration) the ball will backspin up the clubface and into flight.

An upright backswing, with your wrists hinging early, will help produce the sharply descending downswing you desire. Keep your head still and most of your weight on your left foot throughout your swing.

by CLARK P. CHARLES
PROFESSIONAL, VISALIA (CALIF.) COUNTRY CLUB

An open stance for sand shots will cause you to correctly bring your clubhead on an outside-in path on the downswing. The resulting cut shot will make it difficult for you to slice too deeply into the sand.

OPEN STANCE ON BUNKER SHOTS

ALTHOUGH THERE ARE many different ways to execute a shot from a sand bunker, the better golfers always use a slightly open stance.

When addressing the ball, squidge your feet firmly into the sand, keeping the left foot farther than the right from the line of flight. Play the ball well forward in your stance, about opposite your left heel.

With the open stance you'll find it easier to move the clubhead through the sand — and thus make a controlled shot — for two major reasons. First and most important, the open stance makes you swing the clubhead outside the line of flight on the backswing and inside on the downswing. By cutting the shot in this manner the clubhead is less likely to slice too deep and slow down or even stop in the sand. You'll take a thinner cut of sand and this is desirable unless the ball is buried.

Second, the open stance enables the left hip to move well out of the way on the downswing and this helps assure a full follow-through, an important element of the sand trap shot.

by MORGAN FOTTRELL
PROFESSIONAL, ROYAL KAANAPALI G.C., MAUI, HAWAII

Although you normally have a full weight shift to your right foot when hitting with a fairway wood (top), keep your weight on the letf side when hitting with a wood from a fairway trap and restrict your backswing slightly (bottom).

HIT BALL FIRST
FROM FAIRWAY TRAP

IF YOUR BALL SETS up well on top of the sand, you can successfully use a 3-wood or 4-wood from shallow fairway traps. But your clubhead must meet the ball first, before it contacts the sand.

To make sure you hit the ball first, play it back a little farther in your stance than you would on a fairway wood shot. If you play your fairway woods opposite your left heel, play "fairway" trap shots about an inch closer to stance-center. But keep your hands in their normal position. This should put them just forward of the clubhead. This positioning of the ball and your hands will help you bring the clubhead into the ball just before it reaches the lowest part of its arc.

Take a firm stance with your feet, but don't burrow unduly into the sand. This would lower the normal clubhead path and cause your club to dig into the sand.

Your swing should be fairly upright. Use less body turn than normal on the backswing, and by retaining most of your weight on your left foot instead of shifting weight to the right as you would on the fairway.

This upright swing with a minimum of weight shift will help you retain balance in the sand and will also aid you in striking the ball first. Then be sure to complete your swing with a full follow-through.

by ED SUSALLA
PROFESSIONAL, LA COSTA COUNTRY CLUB, ENCINITAS, CALIF.

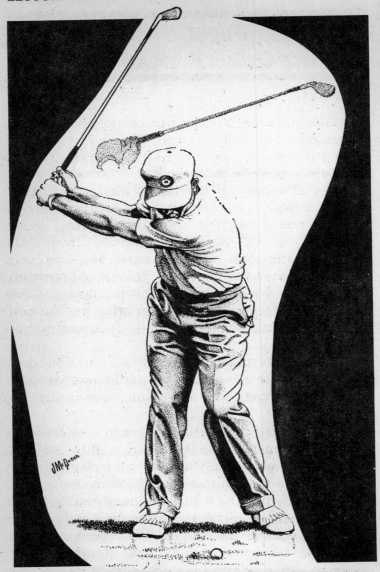

In wet weather take about a 3/4 backswing with every club in your bag.

SWING SHORT IN WET TURF

OREGON GOLFERS, a group with considerable experience in wet-weather golf, recommend a three-quarter backswing, or less, for shots from damp turf.

The short swing is best in wet weather because such a swing makes it easier for the player to make clean contact between club and ball.

The short swing assures maximum control over the club. A golfer is less likely to loosen his grip on a moist clubshaft if he takes a short backswing.

The short backswing also makes it simpler for a player to maintain balance, directly related to clean shots, during his swing.

When employing the short swing in wet weather, you should use a bit more club than normal. Not only does the shorter swing lessen distance, but one can expect little, if any, of his normal roll when the ground is wet.

by LARRY LAMBERGER
PROFESSIONAL, PORTLAND (ORE.) G.C.

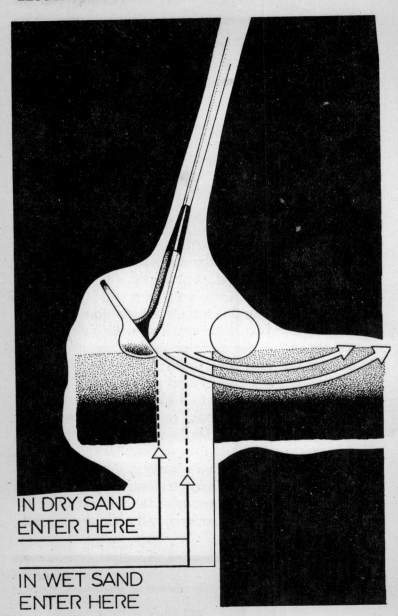

IN DRY SAND
ENTER HERE

IN WET SAND
ENTER HERE

'SHAVE CLOSER' IN WET SAND

THE SALT LAKE COUNTRY CLUB has big traps surrounding most of the greens. The sand is on the powdery side but the traps do get wet after a shower or after sprinklers have watered nearby. Many golfers fear a shot from wet sand, yet it can be made with good results if three things are kept in mind:

1. Make the clubhead enter the sand closer to the ball than you would if playing from dry sand.

2. Swing slightly easier than you would from dry sand.

3. Follow through.

If, when the sand is loose and dry, you ordinarily hit about two inches behind the ball, cut this distance about in half when the sand is wet. Wet sand is heavier and will slow down the clubhead's movement. If you hit too far behind the ball you may bury your club in wet sand and fail to achieve the follow-through that is so important on all sand shots.

Remember, on sand shots *shave closer when wet*, just as you would when shaving your face.

You should also take an easier swing than normal. Wetness packs sand so that a blow of the same force will make the ball fly farther than it would from dry sand. However, remember to finish your swing with a full follow-through.

by TEE BRANCA
PROFESSIONAL, SALT LAKE COUNTRY CLUB, SALT LAKE CITY, UTAH

STRATEGY AND PRACTICE

Intelligent planning — strategy — can in itself make a mediocre game adequate, or an average game excellent. Strategy runs the gamut from the selection of the proper club to figuring the position from which you want to make your next shot.

As commanding as Jack Nicklaus' game is, it's doubtful that he would have reached his current heights were he not such a careful planner. Nicklaus' reputation for "charting" every hole he plays is well known. He goes so far as to carry a notebook with him to mark down the refinements of the course learned in practice rounds.

You need not go so far as Nicklaus, but take a lesson from him. Poor strategy can take the edge off the finest of shots. Before every swing, take a mental survey of the best way to play the shot.

If you play regularly on the same course, become familiar with all of its particular challenges. Know where to drive to your best advantage on every hole, the distances to the green from different landmarks, and the normal speed of every green. Know which are your "attacking" holes — the ones you can do well on. There also may be "defensive" holes that you should play cautiously and conservatively. For example, one a hole traversed by a creek you can carry only with your best tee shot, playing short and then over the water might do the trick safely.

Your strategy can change from round to round. Before you begin a round take a look at the pin locations on holes 9 and 18, usually near the clubhouse. As you play, whenever possible, observe other pin locations before you play those holes. This information could change your strategy on approach shots. Be mentally alert as you play — it'll pay off.

The success of most strategy is dependent on practice. Unless you know what you can do with your clubs, it is impossible to plan intelligently your play for any hole. Learn in practice, not on a course where experimenting can cost you strokes.

Practicing before a round will improve your performance on the course. A session on the practice tee will help you tune-up your body and build coordination. Going "around the clock' 'on the practice putting green will help you develop a sound putting touch that will stay with you through the round.

The lessons in this section are designed for home application. If you are willing to devote the time, they will help you once you are on the course.

*For a high short shot to the green (bottom right),
play the ball forward in your stance to put backspin on the ball. For a fade (top left), open the
clubface slightly and keep your hands well ahead
of the clubhead at address.*

TWO WAYS TO
TAME A 'MONSTER'

Firestone's fabulous 16th hole will always challenge the world's best golfers. Taming this 625-yard monster is a good lesson in golf strategy. I feel there are two ways to par this hole. Each requires a special type of third shot, the mechanics of which will prove to any golfer that there is usually more than one way to beat a long par-5 on almost any course.

If the golfer can drive past the traps on the right side of the fairway, a normal second shot down the left side of the fairway will place him about 80 yards from the green. Here the third shot is an unusually high wedge or 9-iron that will settle quickly on the green.

If, however, the golfer must play short of the traps off the tee, he will probably play his second shot down the right side of the fairway. This will leave him with a third shot of about 150 yards to the right-front side of the green, which is guarded by a pond.

Rather than play over this pond, the more advanced golfer would probably fade a 5- or 6-iron from left to right into the green.

by **ALEX REDL**
PROFESSIONAL, FIRESTONE C.C., AKRON, OHIO

PLAY A DOG-LEG STRAIGHT

IT IS NEARLY always advisable to play a dog-leg hole as a straight hole. Cutting a dog-leg's corner is risky business.

A fine example of the type of hole which should be played without fancy ideas is the 16th at Sea Pines. This 460-yarder is as rugged a par-4 as you can find.

On Sea Pines' 16th, the player who hits straight-away off the tee need only knock the ball 215-225 yards to be in a good approach position. The muscle-man who wants to fly one over the corner must be able to bang it 275 yards. If he just makes it over the trees he must play a needle-sharp approach along the right-hand edge of the fairway. He might even hit it into the rough across the fairway. The straight hitter has a much greater margin for error.

by WALLACE PALMER
PROFESSIONAL, SEA PINES PLANTATION G.C., HILTON HEAD ISLAND, S.C.

PLAY 'SAFE' IN WET WEATHER

PLAYING IN WET weather calls for caution. Water on a clubface often reduces backspin and direction control.

The loss of control in wet weather can be minimized by playing "safe" shots. When making an approach shot, play for the "fat" part of the green and steer clear of possible trouble areas. Make sure your clubface is as dry as possible and sole your club only lightly on the wet grass. Try to catch the ball cleanly without allowing the clubhead to dig into the soft ground.

by JERRY BOYKIN
PROFESSIONAL, LAKEWOOD (OHIO) COUNTRY CLUB

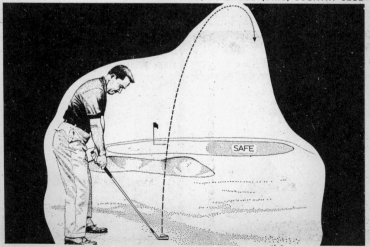

SAFE

CHECK DIVOT MARKS
TO CURE STRAY SHOTS

Your DIVOT MARKS can be very revealing if you are consistently hitting off-line shots. These marks can tell you whether your wildness is due to an improper clubhead path in the hitting area or an improperly positioned clubface at impact.

If your divot marks point straight toward the target, but your shots still stray, the clubface was not looking at the target when it contacted the ball.

However, if your divot mark points to the left of target on shots that pull to the left or slice to the right or to the right on shots that you have pushed in that direction or hooked to the left, your clubhead path is largely at fault.

by JERRY JOHNSTON
PROFESSIONAL, WAIALAE COUNTRY CLUB, HONOLULU, HAWAII

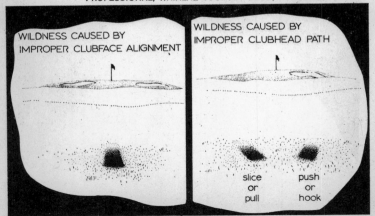

WILDNESS CAUSED BY IMPROPER CLUBFACE ALIGNMENT

WILDNESS CAUSED BY IMPROPER CLUBHEAD PATH

slice or pull

push or hook

SAVE STROKES
WITH MORE CLUB

Everyone makes the mistake of judging distance by the front edge of the green.

Bear in mind that most greens are at least "three clubs" deep. If a 7-iron will reach the front apron, a 6-iron will hit the center of the green and a 5-iron will probably stay on the back edge of the putting surface.

Do not take less club and force the shot, or too much club and shorten your swing. Play for a spot on the green, choose the club that will take your ball there with ease, and swing smoothly.

by PAT ABBOTT
PROFESSIONAL, MEMPHIS (TENN) C.C.

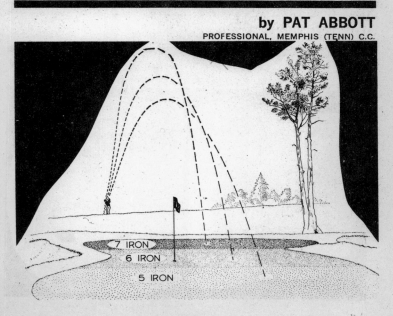

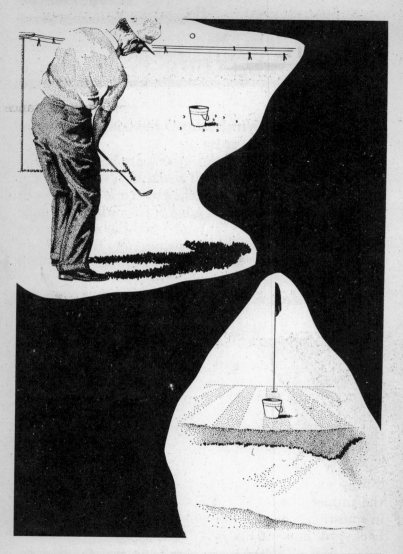

*Developing a "touch" for short chips and pitches
can be done in your own backyard with a bucket.
When you're on the golf course, just imagine that
your landing area on the green is that same bucket.*

DEVELOP ACCURACY IN YOUR OWN BACKYARD

GOLFERS CAN SAVE many strokes during a round if they develop a high degree of "touch" for shots played from just off the edge of the green. Wouldn't it be wonderful if you could miss a green with your approach and still know that you would hole out in two shots?

You can develop an amazingly high degree of skill on short chip and pitch shots by practicing regularly in your backyard. Merely set up a bucket or a basket and practice trying to chip and pitch short shots into it. Make a game of it. See how many of, say, 10 shots you can "sink."

Then when you face short chip and pitch shots during an actual round at the course, merely select the proper "landing spot" on the green for the shot in question, visualize the "bucket" you used in your backyard, and hit the ball "into" it.

by **BOB THOMS**

PROFESSIONAL, RAINBOW SPRINGS COUNTRY CLUB, MUKWONAGO, WIS.

STRENGTHEN LEFT SIDE FOR LONG, ACCURATE SHOTS

A STRONG LEFT SIDE *is* essential if your shots are to have good distance and accuracy. The proper performance of your left side depends largely on the strength of your left wrist and forearm. You can strengthen these with a simple exercise that you can perform while sitting down.

Take a normal grip on a golf club with your left hand only, your thumb on top of the shaft. Then with your left arm and the club fully extended, move them back and forth in front of you in a full half-circle. Your left wrist should not hinge at any time. If you swing the club in this manner at regular intervals you will increase the strength and flexibility of the muscles and tendons in your left wrist and forearm.

by DALE ANDREASON
PROFESSIONAL, PALM SPRINGS (CALIF.) COUNTRY CLUB

'DIAGRAM' SQUARE STANCE BEFORE ADDRESSING BALL

A SQUARE STANCE, in which your feet, hips and shoulders are aligned parallel to the target line, gives you the best chance of hitting the ball straight. A good way to establish a square stance is to diagram it in your imagination as you approach the ball. Then merely fit yourself into the diagram you have visualized as you assume your address position.

Imagine a line from the target running through your ball. Visualize a second line parallel to the first. Then set the toes of your shoes squarely along this second line and check to see that your hips and shoulders are also aligned parallel to the target line.

by DON WARYAN
PROFESSIONAL, HAZELTINE GOLF CLUB, CHASKA, MINN.

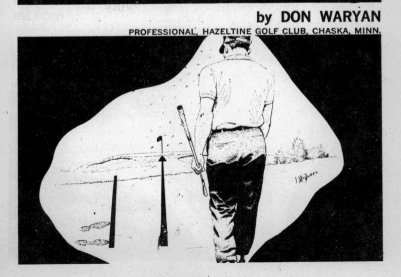

RULES

by JOSEPH C. DEY, JR.

Golf's first written code of rules was established in 1744 by the Company of Gentlemen Golfers (later the Honourable Company of Edinburgh Golfers) who played at the Leith course in Scotland. There were 13 rules then, expressed in 339 words. Today there are 41 rules, encompassing some 15,000 words.

At first glance, this would seem an unnecessarily wordy code for a relatively simple game. However, anyone who has played golf knows that an infinite variety of situations can come up. Actually, the wordage would be even greater if today's rules committee did not strive to minimize the total by legislating in basic principles rather than in minor details whenever it is possible.

In 1897 the Royal and Ancient Golf Club of St. Andrews, Scotland, was acknowledged as the Rules-making authority for all golfers. The United States Golf Association, organized in 1894, followed the R&A code at first, but later began making exceptions, and gradually evolved a distinctive set of Rules. Finally, in 1951 the USGA and the R&A held a conference which produced a world-wide code. Since then the two organizations have met every four years to review and improve the Rules.

The 1968 Rules brought complete uniformity except for golf ball specifications. Both codes fix a maximum weight of 1.62 ounces for the ball, but there are different sizes — the British permit a minimum diameter of 1.62 inches, as compared with the USGA minimum of 1.68 inches. Additionally, the USGA has a requirement concerning velocity — a limit of 250 feet per second when measured on the USGA's apparatus. The R&A does not have any velocity specification.

The introduction of new playing equipment and new trends in the game result in Rules changes at least every four years. An effort, however, is made to keep the game's basic challenges the same and to make them the same for everyone who plays. The Rules revisions for 1968, as an example, ban use of certain croquet type putters and any straddling of the putting line — facing the hole and putting the ball in a "croquet" manner. Both the USGA and the R&A felt that this style of putting was too great a departure from the game's historical concept of striking the ball from the side.

The rules interpretations that follow are a sampling of what you could learn from reading the rule book. A copy may be obtained for 25 cents from the USGA, 40 East 38th Street, New York, N.Y. 10016.

Joseph C. Dey, Jr., executive director of the USGA, has prepared the interpretations included in this section. Dey has exerted great influence on the USGA's Rules Committee since December of 1934, when he came to the national organization.

That year Dey was 27 and his only association with golf had been as an occasional player and as sportswriter for the old *Public Ledger* and the *Evening Bulletin*, both in Philadelphia. But it would seem that his new job and the man were made for each other. Dey is devoted to golf and firmly believes in its principles of fair play.

"The rules are made to help the golfer, not hinder him," Dey says.

As a service to the golfing community, the USGA answers thousands of inquiries every years. These interpretations sometimes cover very unorthodox doings. For instance, there's the golfer (A) who hits the ball into a sand bunker. He carries a rake into the trap and sticks the handle into the sand, intending to use the rake later to smooth the surface. His opponent (B) claims that by doing so, (A) has illegally tested the sand. An official interpretation maintains that (A) indeed has violated the rule and, since they were in match play, loses the hole under Rule 33-1. However, (A) could have carried the rake into the bunker and laid it on the sand. That way he would not be testing the sand.

The rules lessons included in this section are typical of the interpretations offered by the USGA to fit specific situations that golfers everywhere may encounter. Knowing them can save you penalty strokes.

Every serious golfer knows the rules, or at least has a rules book at his disposal. Join the crowd.

AVOID ILLEGAL AID FROM OPPONENT'S CADDIE

PROBLEM: Bill didn't have a caddie. He asked Tom, his opponent, if Tom would let his caddie handle the flagstick occasionally when Bill was on the putting green. Tom consented.

On a green with several undulations between his ball and the hole, Bill asked Tom's caddie two things:

(1) To show him the line of putt by touching the green with a clubhead at a point near the hole, making sure to remove the club before Bill putted:

(2) Whether he should putt boldly or try to make the ball fall softly into the hole.

Was there anything wrong about this?

SOLUTION: Bill breached Rule 9-1 in asking for advice (Definition 2) from his opponent's caddie. Advice may be sought from only the player's own caddie, his partner or his partner's caddie.

Rule 35-1e allows a player to have the line of play shown by anyone on his side, but not by his opponent's caddie. It prohibits touching the line — and that includes touching the green in the manner requested by Bill, even though he did not expect his ball to roll over that exact point.

Penalty for breach of Rules 9 or 35-1e is loss of hole in match play and two strokes in stroke play.

If your ball lies in the fairway resting on a leaf
(loose impediment) or within one club-length of
the leaf, any movement of the ball after the leaf
is removed will cost you a one-stroke penalty.

FALLEN LEAVES —
HANDLE WITH CARE

PROBLEM: The fallen leaf was brown, clearly dead. Part of it appeared to be under Don's ball, although he wasn't sure. He wanted to remove the leaf, but he thought the ball might move in doing so. Don had a vague idea that a penalty might be involved if his ball moved while he removed the leaf. Was he right?

SOLUTION: Being a natural object, the leaf was a loose impediment. Different rules apply, depending on what part of the course the ball lies, as follows:

1. Putting green — No penalty if the ball moves when a loose impediment is removed. The ball must be replaced (Rule 35-1b).

2. Fairway and rough — One stroke penalty if the ball moves after a loose impediment, within one club-length of the ball, has been touched by the player, his partner or either of their caddies. Under Rule 18-2, the player is deemed to have caused the ball to move. The ball is then played from where it came to rest.

3. Hazards — Don is not allowed to touch the leaf in a sand trap or water hazard, even with his club in making his backswing. The penalty is loss of the hole in match play, or two strokes in stroke play (Rule 33-1). However, if the ball is covered by fallen leaves, Don may remove enough of them to enable him to see the top of the ball. If the ball is moved in the process, there is no penalty, but the ball must be replaced (Rule 33-1e).

REPAIR BALL
MARKS ONLY

PROBLEM: On the second green, Sam found problems on his line of putt. First, there was a ball mark, with the bare black earth showing and the turf scarred painfully. Then, near the hole, little flecks of twisted grass testified to the damage which careless players had caused by not lifting their spiked shoes high enough in walking. Close by were little indentations caused by rubber-soled shoes with small gripping features. Finally, there was a sharp, shallow depression made by a mowing machine out of alignment on one side. Could Sam repair all the damage on the line of putt under the Rules of Golf?

SOLUTION: No. He could repair the ball mark (Rule 35-1c), but no other damage. If the Rule allowed repair of spike marks, it would have to distinguish between spike marks and other blemishes — a practical impossibility. In fairness, similar relief would have to be given for marks made by rubber-soled and other shoes, and for spike marks which were merely small holes in the turf that would not affect the roll of the ball. Broadening of the Rule concerning "repair" would probably result eventually in no Rule, opening the way to tampering with and smoothing the line of the putt. This would violate the basic principle. As it is, the line of putt must not be touched except in moving a loose impediment, in repairing ball marks, in lifting a ball for cleaning before the first putt, and in placing the club lightly in front of the ball when addressing it (Rule 35-1a, b, c, d).

DISCARD PROVISIONAL BALL WHEN FIRST IS UNPLAYABLE

PROBLEM: Jimmy knew he had to keep his drive on the right side of the fairway or risk having it kick down a sharp slope to the left into heavy underbrush, and possibly out of bounds. Jimmy's fear came true. His drive hooked left, down the hillside. In his turn, Jimmy teed up another ball and told his opponent he was playing a provisional ball (Rule 30-1a). He played that shot well to the right side of the fairway.

Jimmy found his first ball. It was nestled in the root of a tree, clearly unplayable. "Oh, well," he sighed, "I'll play the provisional ball." Do the rules allow him to do so?

SOLUTION: No. A provisional ball may be played only when the original ball may be out of bounds or lost outside a water hazard. If the original ball is found unplayable, or in a water hazard, the provisional ball must be withdrawn from play (Rule 30-2).

Jimmy had to proceed under Rule 29-2 for an unplayable ball. Under penalty of one stroke, he could either (1) drop a ball behind the unplayable lie so as to keep that spot between himself and the hole, going back as far as he wanted; (2) drop a ball within two club-lengths of the unplayable lie, but not nearer the hole, or (3) play again from the tee (stroke-and-distance penalty).

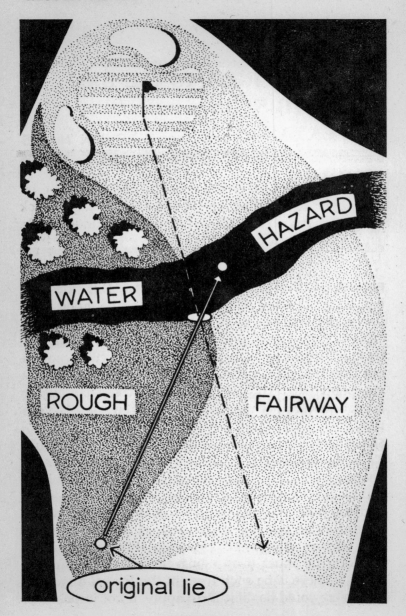

HAZARD

WATER

ROUGH

FAIRWAY

original lie

DROP IN PROPER SPOT FROM WATER HAZARD

PROBLEM: In playing from the rough, Bill skies his ball and it lands in a brook in front of the green — in an unplayable lie. He wants to drop a ball along his "line of flight" and take a stroke penalty, but to do so he must drop in the rough. His opponent, Tom, points out that Bill may drop a ball in the fairway if he keeps the point where his first ball last crossed the water hazard margin between himself and the hole. Is Tom right?

SOLUTION: Yes. If Bill elects to proceed under Rule 33-2a, he must drop a ball behind the water hazard, keeping the spot where his ball last crossed the hazard as the margin between the position of his drop and the hole. He may drop as far behind the water hazard as he desires. If this enables him to drop in the fairway, that's his privilege. Bill is wrong in thinking he must drop along the so-called "line of flight." There is no such term in the Rules. Any such provision would be difficult to apply, if not impossible.

WHEN ONE BALL MOVES ANOTHER IN MATCH PLAY

PROBLEM: In a four-ball match, in which two play their better ball against the better ball of two other players, Jack and Jerry are playing Tom and Tony.

Jack's ball is lying close to the hole. Tom putts and his ball knocks Jack's ball farther away from the hole. Jack replaces his ball over the protests of Tom and Tony. Who is right?

SOLUTION: Jack must replace his ball, without penalty. In a four-ball match, if a ball moves any other ball, the owner of the moved ball is obliged to replace it (Rule 40-1c). In a single match — one player against one other — the owner of such a moved ball may either replace it or leave it where it comes to rest; he must decide before either player plays again (Rule 35-2c).

GRANT RELIEF FROM CASUAL WATER ON GREEN

PROBLEM: Casual water could be seen on almost the entire green as Jack came up to his ball. The water seemed deepest directly on Jack's line of putt. About five feet to the left, the putting line was clear of standing water, and the ball of Harry, Jack's opponent, was in that area. This was a new situation for Jack, and he didn't know what to do. He had an idea he could move his ball from the deepest water but, on second thought, he had doubts about his rights because there was scarcely any line to the hole without casual water on it. What were Jack's rights?

SOLUTION: Jack was entitled to relief without penalty because casual water lay between his ball and the hole on the green. He had the right to lift his ball and place it in the nearest position which afforded maximum relief from the casual water, but which was not nearer the hole. (Rules 32-1c, 32-2; Definition 8). Harry was already in the position which afforded maximum relief from the casual water, and so he was obliged to play his ball as it lay. Other applications of the rules affording relief occur if the ball lies in or touches casual water, or if casual water interferes with the player's stance.

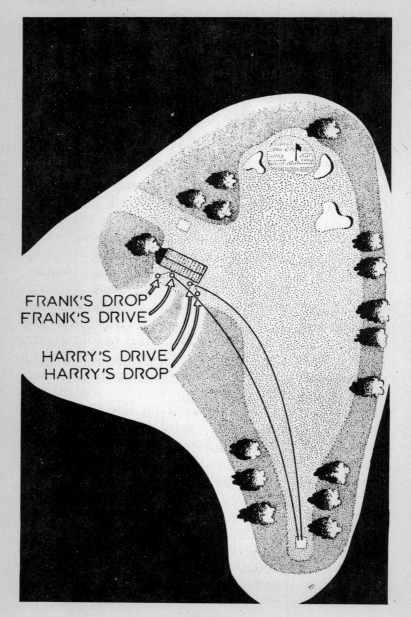

FRANK'S DROP
FRANK'S DRIVE

HARRY'S DRIVE
HARRY'S DROP

'RELIEF' FROM OBSTRUCTION NEED. NOT PROVIDE CLEAR SHOT

PROBLEM: Harry and Frank, who didn't know much about the Rules, both hooked their drives and found their balls about a foot behind a shelter shed which blocked their direct lines to the hole. They were about to play their shots as they lay when their "double" caddie pointed out that the shelter, being artificial, was an obstruction. Since it interfered with both their swings, they could have free drops away from the shelter, according to Rule 31-2. The caddie guided them in dropping away, each within two club lengths of the nearest point of the obstruction, in any direction but not nearer the hole than their original lies. Harry's free drop gave him a clear line to the hole. Frank, however, was still blocked out after his drop, and he did not think this fair in view of Harry's relief. Is Frank's complaint justified under the Rules?

SOLUTION: No. The purpose of Rule 31-2 is to give the player opportunity to *swing the club* without interference from an obstruction, if that is possible. The Rule is not concerned with whether relief gives the player a good or bad "break." As the Rule says, "Interference with the line of play is not of itself interference under this Rule."

LEAVE NATURE ALONE IN HAZARD

PROBLEM: Your ball stops in a rather untidy bunker. An empty soft drink bottle is lying a few inches in front of your ball and a good-sized twig, fallen from a nearby tree, is behind your ball. To play your ball as it lies, your club will strike the twig first, then the ball and perhaps will follow through into the bottle. What are your rights if any?

SOLUTION: (A) The twig, being natural, is a loose impediment. Since it lies in a hazard it may not be touched or moved before your club swings forward for the stroke (Rule 33-1).

(B) The bottle, being artificial, is an obstruction. As such, it may be removed from the hazard without penalty (Rule 31-1).

REMOVABLE

NON-REMOVABLE

PROPER PROCEDURE
WHEN BALL IS LOST

PROBLEM: Pete's tee shot sliced off the fairway into underbrush on the right. After a short search, Pete started to walk back to the tee to hit a second shot, remarking that his ball must be lost. Then a caddie found Pete's ball, less than five minutes after the search had begun. Pete returned to play it, but John, his playing companion, said he couldn't do so since he had abandoned the original ball by starting back to the tee. Was John right?

SOLUTION: No. Pete was entitled to play his original ball from where it lay since it was found within five minutes of searching and before he had put another ball into play (Definition 6).

Had Pete's ball been lost, he would have had to return to the spot from where the shot had been played — in this case, the tee — to hit another ball. He would then count both strokes and add a penalty stroke for the lost ball (Rule 29-1). Thus he would be shooting three from the tee.

發行人：陳　　明　　仁
住　址：台北市迪化街二段二四三巷七號
發行所：光　輝　出　版　社
經銷處：僑　裕　有　限　公　司
印刷所：光達印刷廠有限公司
廠　址：台北縣景美鎮萬盛里公館街一號
中華民國五十七年　　月　　日第一版
・登記證：內版台業字第一三二號・